Character Wreaths

12 Holiday Projects for Year 'Round Décor

Kasey Rogers & Mark Wood

Published by

krause publications

700 East State Street • Iola, WI 54990-0001
715/445-2214 • FAX: 715/445-4087   www.krause.com

Please call or write for our free catalog of publications. Our toll-free number to place an order or obtain a free catalog is 800-258-0929.

Library of Congress Catalog Number: 2001096275

ISBN: 0-87349-380-X

The following registered and trademarked company and product names appear in this publication: A D Velasco, Aleene's® (Duncan Enterprises), The Beistle Co.®, Bel Tree Dolly Eyes®, Bumples Brand Doll Hair®, Dap-Tex® Insulation Foam Sealant, DBD Enterprises (Designs by Dian), The Egypt Store, Goldberger Doll Mfg. Co., Inc., Hammerite Spray Paints™, Integrity Toys, Inc.™, Kinko's, Inc.™, Modern Options® Sophisticated Finishes™, Paper Mart, Polymark Paints™, Styrofoam Brand Foam™ by Dow Chemical Co.™, Wright's Trim®.

Introduction

Mark Wood and Kasey Rogers.

Several years ago, while faced with having to make yet another wreath, Kasey and I sat staring at an empty straw ring. What could we do that would be different? Well, it was autumn and a scarecrow came to mind. After all, scarecrows are stuffed with straw. Then it all fell into place. The ring could become "arms" with the help of a sleeve and a pair of old gloves, and the head could be made from something as basic as an old feed sack. How easy! Thus was born our first character wreath. We made several. They could be made to hold dishes or decorations. And then it hit us again… wreaths could be made into any holiday character imaginable! In this book, Kasey and I show you how to make a character wreath for every month of the year.

- Mark D. Wood

P.S. The instructions for our scarecrow wreath can be found in our book, *Halloween Crafts: Eerily Elegant Décor*, another great Krause publication.

Thank Yous

Kasey and Mark would like to thank the wonderful people who opened the doors of their historic locations to us:

David Dickson at Union Station, Los Angeles (PH: 213-617-0111)
Phyllis Power at Calabasas Park
Caroline Asencio of the Avilla Adobe-Olvera St., Los Angeles (PH: 213-625-5045)
Theresa Castillo of the Veterans Administration, Los Angeles (Wadsworth Chapel)
Sandra Hildebrandt of the Stagecoach Inn Museum, Newbury Park, CA (PH: 805-498-9441)
William Livingston of the Los Angeles National Cemetery (PH: 310-268-4494)
Barbara Smith of American Cinemateque/Grauman's Egyptian Theatre, Hollywood, CA (PH: 323-467-0434)
Ann Dorr of the Durfee House Bed and Breakfast Inn, Los Angeles, CA (PH: 213-748-1996)

Thanks also go out to Amy Tincher-Durik, Barbara Case, and all the great people at Krause Publications and to our families and friends for all their help and support in getting this book out of our heads and onto the bookstore shelves!

Table of Contents

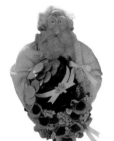

Basic Supplies

- straw wreath: 10", 12", or 14" diameter
- sewing machine
- needle and thread
- scissors
- iron
- hot glue gun
- lots of glue sticks
- quilt pins
- 2" nails
- packing tape
- small hand saw
- drill with 1-1/2" bit (optional, or as specified in project instructions)
- needle nose pliers

The Golden Rule

Quilt pins are your friends! They help hold everything in place, from heads to hands, sleeves to entire floral arrangements. Just be sure they are well glued and seated into the straw wreath.

Preparing the Wreath

1. To form the "arms" of the straw wreath, tightly wrap a 3"-wide area with packing tape.

2. Saw the wreath in two at the middle of the taped area.

3. Tape each raw end tightly closed. Trim away any nylon thread ends that have been cut.

4. Depending on the type of head you use for your wreath, you may need to drill a hole in the wreath. Generally, the head will require a 1-1/2" neck hole in the center top of the wreath. After drilling the hole, clean out any straw debris with needle nose pliers and clip all the nylon threads. Refer to the project instructions for more specific directions.

Wreath Wreminder

The nylon threads wrapped around straw wreaths will wrap themselves tightly around your drill bit. Be sure to cut them loose often.

Wreath Wreminder

*Heads are always attached to the wreaths **after** the appropriate sleeve has been put on.*

Heads and Faces

The following instructions are for the different types of heads used in the projects in this book. Don't feel limited to use the same ones we did – all heads are interchangeable.

Tube Sock Head

Using a tube sock makes this soft-sculpture head super-easy.

The side view of a tube sock head.

Instructions

1. Tightly stuff a tube sock with fiberfill to form an oval ball large enough for the head, roughly 5" x 6". When the fiberfill is firmly compacted, tie a knot in the sock at the bottom of the head.

2. Tie a piece of string around the sock ball at the eye line. Pull the string tight to form an indention and knot it in the back. Trim the string ends close to the knot.

3. Tie the middle of another piece of string tightly around the knot at the bottom of the sock (this will help hold it in place). Join the two ends at the top of the head and pull tight. Knot and clip the string ends.

> **The tube sock head was used for:**
> * Cinco de Mayo (page 18)
> **You will need:**
> - tube sock
> - fiberfill
> - 1/2 yd. rib-knit fabric (appropriate skin tone)
> - ball of cotton string
> - skein embroidery floss (eye color)
> - embroidery needle
> - 1-3/4" wooden dowel, at least 7"-long

4. Where the two strings meet at the sides of the head, take a couple of stitches to secure them to the sock. Slide the knot at the top of the head down the back of the head. If this string is loose, unknot it and tie it tighter, again trimming off the thread ends.

Wreath Wreminder

Many times it's difficult to tell if the head is the right size for your wreath until it has been tied off like this. If it's too big, untie the sock and pull out some fiberfill. If it's too small, carefully cut off the strings, add fiberfill, and retie the head.

5. Cut a circle of rib-knit fabric large enough to completely encircle the sock ball. Stitch a gathering stitch around the outside edge of the fabric. Place the fabric over the top of the ball and tighten it around the sock knot at the bottom of the head. Pull the gathering thread tight and tie it off.

Wreath Wreminder

You don't want any "play" in the rib-knit fabric. If it's too loose, cut the gathering thread and gather it again a little further up from your first set of stitches.

6. The eyes are created with satin stitches using embroidery floss. For the most part the faces we created for the book are suggestions. We chose not to put noses and mouths on ours and to let the elaborateness of the wreath show instead, but a stitched mouth and a small nose made of rib knit is always a possibility!

7. To secure the head to the wreath, untie the knot in the sock at the bottom of the head and insert the 7" wooden dowel deep into the head. Add some hot glue in the hole to secure. Then use scissors points to make a starter hole through the sleeve and into the wreath. Put some hot glue in the hole and insert the dowel.

Nylon Stocking Head

Mark first taught how to make these heads when he was in high school and they were first becoming popular... just last year! Ha!

The nylon stocking head was used for:
* Uncle Sam (page 24)
* School Ma'arm (page 28)

You will need:
* knee-high nylon stocking, skin tone
* fiberfill
* ladies powdered blush

Instructions

1. Stuff the nylon stocking with fiberfill to make a ball approximately 6" or 7" in diameter. Determine which is the best side for a face. (Usually the lumps of fiberfill will give a good indication.) Add a small wad of fiberfill for the nose. Tuck a "roll" of fiberfill under the nose from ear to ear to form the beginning of a chin.

2. Tie a tight knot in the stocking below the fiberfill, turn upside down, and bring the remaining stocking back up over the head for added strength and color. Tie a knot in the stocking end and trim off the excess.

3. Double thread a large needle with off-white thread. (To double the thread, pull off a good length of thread and bring the two ends together. Thread both ends through the eye of the needle and bring all four ends together and knot.) You'll need this extra thread strength because you are going to pull it very tight.

4. Insert the needle into the top of the head near the knot and bring it out where one eye would be. Go back in with the needle, creating about a 1/2" stitch and come out where the other eye will be. Make another 1/2" stitch and come back out at the top of the head.

5. Repeat twice, pulling tightly as you go to create two indentations for the eyes. Take a couple of stitches at the top of the head and tie off the thread.

6. Form a nose by pinching a triangle in the stocking and fiberfill. Insert the needle and thread through the top of the head and bring it out on the right side of the nose. Make a 1/2" stitch and bring the needle out on the left side of the nose. Be sure to dig deeply under the wad of fiberfill that forms the nose. Repeat the stitch on the left side and bring the needle out on the right side of the nose. Pull the thread tight. Reinsert the needle on the right side of the nose and bring it out the top of the head. Pull the thread tight and tie it off.

7. Again insert the needle through the top of the head and exit where one

nostril will be. Take a 1/4" stitch and come back out the top of the head, pulling tight to create an indentation. Repeat for the second nostril. Tie off the thread.

8. To create the mouth, insert the threaded needle from under the neck and bring it out at the top of the chin, about 3/4" below the nostrils and a little off-center.

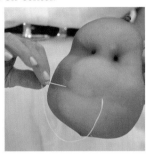

9. Take a horizontal stitch about 1" long and go back in the other side of the mouth and exit at the bottom of the chin. Do this twice more, pulling the thread as you go. Take a few small stitches under the chin and tie off the thread.

10. At this stage, the face should be taking on human characteristics, depending on how tightly you've pulled the thread. Use the needle to reach deep inside and manipulate the fiberfill to puff up the cheeks and chin. Be careful when doing this – if you prick the outside of the stocking you may put a run in your face! How hard you pull the threads and how often you fluff will change the look of your face.

11. Apply a little powdered blush to the cheeks, chin, and forehead to add realism to your stocking face.

12. At this point, the head can become anything from a Santa Claus to a witch to a grandparent. Choose which character you want to create and decorate the head appropriately. After the head is decorated and the sleeve put on, attach it to the wreath. Add a good supply of hot glue and set the head on top of the wreath. Holding the head in place while the glue is still warm, imbed three or four quilt pins through the nylon around the base of the head and into the straw. Make sure these pins are well seated in the straw.

Wreath Wreminder
It may seem logical to use a dowel to attach the nylon stocking head, but don't. If you accidentally make a hole in the stocking, you risk a big run in the face.

Photo Transfer Head

Did you know? Certain forms of transferring photos to fabric have been in use for well over a hundred years! Today, photo transfers have grown in popularity from only being used on t-shirts to being found on everything from quilts to pillowcases! This head is one of the simplest to do.

The photo transfer head was used for:
* Santa Claus (page 34)
You will need:
• 1/3 yd. white muslin
• photo or drawing
• fiberfill

Instructions

1. Take your favorite photograph or drawing to a Kinko's or other copy store and have a heat transfer made from it. Make sure they first enlarge the photo (hair and all) to the appropriate size. Most heads for these wreaths need to be 5" to 7" when finished.

2. Cut the muslin in half and iron the transfer onto one half.

3. Place the two muslin pieces right sides together and cut out the transferred head, adding a 1-1/2" border all around. Machine stitch around the fabric edge with a 1/4" seam allowance. Leave the bottom of the head/neck open for stuffing and turning. Clip notches close to the stitch line for smooth curves. Turn right side out.

4. Stuff with fiberfill. Be careful not to overstuff or you will distort the facial features. Topstitch the neck area shut very close to the stuffing to hold it in place. Trim away any excess fabric.

5. This head is attached to the wreath with hot glue and quilt pins. Use a good supply of hot glue to attach the head on top of the wreath and hold the head in place until the glue sets. Do not put pins in the front of the head because they can distort the image.

Doll Heads and Masks

Vinyl doll heads.

Perhaps the easiest head of all is to find a readymade doll head to place on your wreath. This is not nearly as easy as it sounds. Today, few dolls are made with large enough heads (5" to 7"). However, we were lucky enough to come up with a few great sources, which are listed in Wreathsources on page 48. These companies sell doll heads and masks that are lovely, whimsical, and perfect for you to use. Doll heads and masks are available in porcelain, vinyl, or hard plastic.

You will need:
• doll mask or head
• Styrofoam ball same size as mask (for masks only)
• doll hair (if not already on the head)
• white glue
• 3/4" wooden dowel, 7"-long (or as specified in project instructions)
The mask head was used for:
* Father Time (page 10)
* Leapin' Leprechauns (page 14)
* Miss Liberty (page 26)
* Mum's the Word (page 30)
The doll head was used for:
* Queen of Hearts (page 12)
* Bunny Baby (page 16)
* Indian Maiden (page 32)

Instructions

1. If using a **vinyl doll mask**, wedge a Styrofoam ball into the back of the mask and secure it with hot glue. You can later add hair, a hood, or a hat around this base. Attach it to the wreath by pushing 2" nails through the back of the mask and into the wreath. Position the mask with the chin resting on the front of the wreath and further secure the nails with hot glue.

2. If using a **porcelain doll mask**, wedge a Stryrofoam ball into the back of the mask and secure it with hot glue. Attach this to the wreath with a wooden dowel. Use scissors points to bore a hole in the wreath and insert the dowel into the hole, then into the Styrofoam ball and secure with hot glue. Remember that the head isn't mounted until after the sleeve is on the wreath.

3. If using a **hard plastic mask** like those in Miss Liberty (page 26) and Mum's the Word (page 30), first trim 1/2" from around the edge of the mask with scissors, then glue the mask to a Styrofoam ball with white glue (hot glue will melt the mask). Use scissors points to bore a hole in the wreath and insert the dowel into the hole, then into the Styrofoam ball. Secure with hot glue.

4. If using a vinyl **doll head** with a neck, secure the head to the wreath by drilling a hole in the top of the wreath large enough to accommodate the neck. Fill the hole with hot glue and insert the neck firmly in place.

Wreath Wreminder
Position the chin even with the inside rim of the wreath, not perched on top.

5. Some **porcelain doll heads** come with an arched shoulder/neck. These are easily attached to the wreath by hot gluing the underside of the shoulder/neck to the wreath and inserting tiny 1-1/2" nails (with heads) through the stitch holes provided in the shoulder/neck.

Sleeves, Cuffs, and Lapels

You will cover the "arms" of each wreath with some sort of fabric sleeve. Depending on the project you choose, you might also add cuffs and lapels. Because the thickness and circumference of straw wreaths vary, the sleeve measurements given on the pattern templates are approximate. Follow the directions below to find the precise measurements for your wreath.

Measuring for the Sleeve

1. Measure the outside wreath circumference and add 3" to 5" for hems and "play." This is the fabric length.

2. Measure around the thickness of the wreath and add 3" to 5" for fullness. This is the fabric width.

Tube Sleeve and Bow Tie Sleeve

While these two sleeves look different when finished, the sewing instructions are the same for both.

> **The tube sleeve was used for:**
> * Leapin' Leprechauns (page 14)
> * Bunny Baby (page 16)
> * Groom (page 20)
> * School Ma'arm (page 28)
> * Indian Maiden (page 32)
>
> **The bow tie sleeve was used for:**
> * Father Time (page 10)
> * Miss Liberty (page 26)
>
> **For the tube sleeve you will need:**
> * 1/3 yd. fabric
> * 1/3 yd. lining fabric (if necessary)

Tube Sleeve

The tube sleeve is a breeze to make. It's a simple fabric rectangle, approximately 12" x 45", sewn into a tube. For a precise measurement, refer to the measuring instructions on this page. Sometimes the tube sleeve is lined, but that's not usually necessary.

Bow Tie Sleeve

The bow tie sleeve looks like a choir robe when it's finished. Use the illustration to create a paper pattern piece the correct size. The measurements shown are approximate. For precise measurements, refer to the measuring instructions on this page. Cut one from outer fabric and one from lining. *Note:* Since the interior of these sleeves shows, they should always be lined.

> **For the bow tie sleeve you will need:**
> * 3/4 yd. fabric
> * 3/4 yd. lining fabric

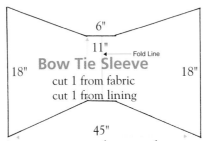

6"

11" — Fold Line

18"   **Bow Tie Sleeve**   18"
cut 1 from fabric
cut 1 from lining

45"

enlarge to measurements shown or to fit your wreath

Instructions

1. Cut a piece of fabric, either in a rectangle to fit your wreath or using the Bow Tie Sleeve pattern. (If the project you choose requires the sleeve to be lined, skip to Step 4.)
2. With right sides together, stitch along the entire long edge of the sleeve. Press the seam open
3. Turn the cuff ends up twice to hem and press. Stitch the hems and turn the sleeve right side out. If you aren't lining the sleeve, skip to Step 7.
4. If you are lining the sleeve, cut one sleeve of outer fabric and one of lining. Cut the lining in half at the fold line.
5. With right sides together, stitch the lining to the outer fabric at each cuff. Press the seams open.

After stitching each lining piece to each cuff end, pin at the seams, sleeve center, and each end.

With right sides together, fold the outer sleeve and lining lengthwise and pin it in a tube at the cuff seams, center, and each end. Stitch along the entire length of the seam. Remove the pins and press the seam open.

6. Pull each lining piece back over the outer sleeve and whipstitch the lining back together at the center seam.

After stitching the entire sleeve (including both lining pieces) from end to end, pull the lining pieces back over the outer sleeve to meet at the center.

Whipstitch the lining back together at the center cut. Be careful not to catch the outer sleeve.

Turn the entire sleeve right side out. Press the ends of the sleeves smooth.

Pull the sleeve right side out and lightly press.

7. Slide the sleeve onto the wreath.

The finished tube sleeve, ready to be slid on the wreath.

Sweater Knit Tube Sleeve

Here's a variation of the fabric tube sleeve for those of you who like to knit.

Instructions

Cast on 28 stitches.
For the ribbed cuff:
Rows #1 through #12, k2, p2.
Row #13, k4, increase one stitch.
Repeat five more times to 34 stitches, approximately 9"

For the sleeve body:
Row #14, k.
Row #15, p.
Continue k a row, p a row until sleeve measures 28" overall.
To decrease for the second ribbed cuff, k4, k2 together and repeat five more times, returning to 28 stitches.
For the second cuff:
The last 12 rows repeat the first 12 rows in a k2, p2 pattern, matching the first ribbed cuff.
Bind off, leaving about 36" of yarn attached. Thread the attached yard through the embroidery needle and join the seams lengthwise by whipstitching them together.
Slip the sleeve on the wreath with the seam at the back. Push the sleeve up at each end, leaving 1-1/2" of the wreath bare on each cuff. This will leave room for the embellishments you add later while still allowing the ribbed cuffs to show.
Cut a neck hole in the center top of the knit sleeve. When you hot glue the head to the wreath, the hot glue will fuse the cut knit edges and keep the knit sleeve from unraveling.

Sport Coat Sleeve and Lapels with Dress Shirt Collar and Cuffs

Visit a thrift shop or go through your closet to find an old sport coat and dress shirt. These can be easily and inexpensively transformed into sleeves for a multitude of character wreaths.

Instructions

1. Remove the sleeves from the sport coat by cutting the stitching at the arm holes. Remove any padding in the shoulders of the jacket until you are left with just the sleeve and its lining. Topstitch the lining to the sleeve to hold it in place.
2. Remove the jacket lapels by cutting them from the jacket near, but not on, the press line (where the lapel was originally folded over and pressed). This will allow the lapels to still fold over and hide all the raw edges.

Wreath Wreminder

Make sure you put the proper sleeve on the correct side of the wreath (left on left, right on right). Always let the shirt cuffs show from under the sport coat sleeves and be sure the cuff and jacket sleeve buttons show.

3. Cut the cuffs off the old dress shirt about 5" up from the bottom edge. Slip each cuff onto the wreath arms, letting the finished cuff edge touch the cut edge of the wreath. Secure the cuff to the wreath by wrapping packing tape around the top cut edge of the cuff. The tape will be hidden once the jacket sleeves are on.
4. Slide the sport coat sleeves onto the wreath and position them in place with one sleeve overlapping the other at the top. Fold under the excess sleeve on top and hold it in place with quilt pins. Whipstitch the front and back of the sleeves together.
5. Cut the collar and the shirt front or "placket" from the shirt. Cut the back of the collar close to the stitch line. Leave a lot of excess material on the shirt front, starting at the shoulder seam. This can be trimmed away later.

6. Attach the head to the wreath before continuing. (Refer to the directions for the type of head you made for attaching instructions.) Be sure to leave a small bit of "neck" showing. Once this is done, unbutton the collar and shirt front to position it around the head and button it again.
7. Place a 5" x 5" square of cardboard under the shirt front and glue it to the wreath. This will keep the shirt placket stiff and in place. Hot glue the shirt edges down on the cardboard.
8. Bring the sport coat lapels around the shirt collar and overlap them in front. Once you are happy with the position of the lapels, hot glue them to the wreath, starting with a couple drops around the neck and shirt collar and then onto the placket. Trim away any excess shirt and cardboard that may be showing. Cut away the excess from the underside lapels. Fold the overlapped lapel points under, hiding all the raw edges, and stitch to hold.

Floral Arrangements

We often separate large flower clusters such as hydrangeas and geraniums into tiny individual blossoms and we usually clip artificial flowers and leaves from their stems and bushes.

Create your own arrangements by hot gluing the individual flowers and leaves together. Remember, anything you put together will look better than stiff store-bought flowers. Study our floral arrangements to see how they were constructed.

You can bore small holes through the sleeve and into the straw wreath with scissors or an ice pick to hold silk flower stems and hot glue them in place.

Hanging Your Wreath

One of the best ways to hang character wreaths is with a large saw-toothed picture hanger attached to the wreath with long nails and hot glue. Or, sink a screw eye deep into the wreath behind the character's head. Another great hanging idea is to make several stitches with embroidery floss around a pencil at the back of the neck. When you remove the pencil, you're left with hanging loops.

January

Father Time and Baby New Year

You will need:

- 14" straw wreath
- # ST901 vinyl Santa mask with beard, DBD Ent.*
- 10" vinyl baby doll
- top hat with feather to fit doll's head
- antique white felt – 2 yd. 36"-wide or 1 yd. 72"-wide
- pkg. crystal color seed pearl beads
- pkg. 6mm silver sequin stars
- pkg. 1/2" silver sequin stars
- beading needle
- white glue
- florist wire
- wire cutters
- pliers
- black marker
- 3/8" wooden dowel, 15"-long
- empty black champagne bottle with cork (label removed)
- 2 pkgs. 20" silver wire floral sticks (60 total)
- 15 sprays 1" clear glass Christmas ornaments, separated
- 15 sprays 1/2" clear glass Christmas ornaments, separated
- several nonworking pocket watches (found in thrift stores or online)

*see Wreathsources, page 48

Midnight, New Year's Eve – that fateful moment sealed with a kiss, when the old bids goodbye and welcomes the new.

Instructions

1. Prepare the wreath as directed on page 5.

2. Prepare the purchased vinyl Santa head for mounting as directed on page 7. Do not mount the head yet.

Hood and Sleeve

1. Find the pattern for Father Time's Hood on page 36. Make a paper pattern the right size and cut two from felt. Use a 1/4" seam allowance to stitch around the top and sides as shown on the pattern. Leave the bottom open for turning. Turn right side out and push point A in to meet point B. The seams will now be together at the back of the hood. Topstitch the bottom opening closed.

2. The bow tie sleeve is also made from felt. Find the pattern and sewing instructions on page 8. Because this sleeve is made from felt, it does not need to be lined. Slide the finished sleeve on the wreath and turn the cuffs back.

3. Re-tape the wreath ends together.

4. To bead the stars, single thread a beading needle and knot the thread. Bring the needle up through the sleeve. Add a sequin star (either size) and a pearl bead and return the needle through the same hole in the sequin. Re-enter the felt where the thread originally came out. Exit the felt where you wish to place the next sequin star. Pull taut. The bead will hold the sequin star in place. Do this in a random pattern around the shoulders and cuffs. The more the merrier!

5. Attach the mask head to the wreath as directed on page 7.

6. Hot glue the fabric hood to the mask forehead and around the shoulders. Sew more beaded stars around the hood.

Finishing Touches

1. To mount the baby, cut a small hole in the top of the doll's head and in the doll's bottom (ouch!). Insert the 15" wooden dowel through the entire doll, allowing equal lengths to stick out of the top and bottom. Hot glue the top hat to the doll's head by gluing it to the dowel. (Most glues will not stick to vinyl baby dolls.)

2. Cut a slit through the sleeve and into the wreath on Father Time's left shoulder and push the dowel into the straw. Secure with hot glue. Remove the wires from a few glass ornaments and hot glue them around the base of the doll and to the top hat.

3. Create a New Year's label for the champagne bottle by photocopying the art on page 36. Cut out the label and use white glue to affix it to the bottle.

4. Bend the 60 florist wire sticks in half. Crimp them together with pliers and wedge them about 1" deep into the bottle opening. Slightly fan out the wires.

5. Wire the glass ornaments in sprays of five and six, using both sizes in each spray. Insert the wire ends of the ornament sprays into the florist wire sticks and secure with hot glue. Continue until all the florist wires are covered and a canopy of ornaments has been created.

6. Using wire cutters, carefully apply pressure to the base of several of the remaining 1/2" glass ornaments and break off the bases (wear protective eye covering when working with glass).

7. Add hot glue all around the broken ends and affix them to the tops of some of the larger glass ornaments for depth (see the photo). Save a few glass ornament sprays for decorating the wreath.

8. Drip some hot glue around the top of the champagne bottle to look like spilling champagne and to help hold the wires steady.

9. Attach the bottle to the arms of Father Time by wrapping a piece of florist wire around the base of the bottle and securing it to the wreath with a 2" nail embedded deep into the straw. Secure the nail with hot glue. Use a black marker to color the wire to match the bottle. Add another nail through the base of the wire spray and into the wreath. Again, secure with hot glue.

10. Add the last remaining glass "bubbles" around the bottom of the bottle. Hot glue them in place. Arrange the pocket watches (all hands should be placed at five minutes to midnight!) around the wreath and secure them with hot glue.

11. Use white glue to adhere more silver sequin stars around the glass balls and in Father Time's beard.

12. As a final touch, we glued a few stray glass bubbles around the bottle's cork, stuck the cork on a wire, and inserted it into the mass of glass bubbles on the top.

Did You Know?

According to early calendars, New Year's Eve was once celebrated at the end of October. Wow, what would we do with Hallowe'en?

Father Time was photographed at a clock tower on famous Melrose Avenue in Los Angeles.

February

Queen of Hearts

The Queen of Hearts was photographed at the park in old town Calabasas in the midst of her pink and white flower-filled garden. She holds her tray of tarts just recently recovered from that thieving knave.

Instructions

1. Prepare the wreath as directed on page 5.

2. Prepare the vinyl doll head as directed on page 7. Do not attach the head to the wreath yet.

Sleeve

1. Find the pattern for the Queen of Hearts Sleeve on page 37. Make a paper pattern piece the right size and cut one of velvet and one of quilted flannel. Pin the two pieces wrong sides together with the velvet laying on top of the flannel.

2. Single thread the beading needle and knot it. Bring the needle up through the velvet at the point where the quilted diamond patterns intersect. Add a pearl bead and re-enter the velvet next to where the thread originally came out. Repeat at every quilted intersection. Randomly exchange a pearl bead for a red sequin heart. Attach the hearts by bringing the needle up through it, adding a seed pearl and re-entering the heart and fabric at the same place.

3. Once beaded and with right sides together, stitch the sleeve (with its lining) together lengthwise. Turn right side out and slip it onto the wreath with the seam on the outside edge.

4. Re-tape the cut wreath ends together.

5. Hot glue the pre-gathered lace trim around the raw cuff edges. Cover the lace edges with a length of the red braid trim.

Head, Crown, and Earrings

1. Most vinyl doll heads come with hair. The "Dancie" head we used came with a ponytail. We undid it and inserted a little batting in the hair for a "rat" and some hairpins to put her hair in an "up-do" on top of her head. It takes some work to keep artificial hair from separating but it's well worth it!

2. Trace or photocopy the pattern for the Queen of Hearts Crown on page 37 and cut a crown out of thin cardboard. Paint the crown red inside and out. Hot glue pearl trim along the bottom of the crown and on all the hearts along the top of the crown. Hot glue a red filigree heart to the middle three hearts on the crown and to the center bottom point. Top the filigree hearts with a long pearl drop bead by removing the gold hanger on the bead and hot gluing it in place.

3. Wrap the crown around the hair bun (which will help hold it in place) and hot glue the back ends together. If needed, a quilt pin may be inserted through the crown and into the vinyl head to hold it in place.

4. Paint the ends of two quilt pins red and thread a pearl drop bead on each. Insert a pin into each earlobe of the doll's head. A tiny, black beauty mark made with a marker or paint pen is a very grownup touch on this lovely doll.

Collar

1. Trace or photocopy the pattern for the Queen of Hearts Collar on page 38 and cut two of red felt and one of interfacing.

2. Place the two felt pieces right sides together, then place the interfacing on top. Stitch around all edges with a 1/4" seam allowance, leaving an opening for turning. Clip all curves and turn right side out. Hand stitch the opening closed and press.

3. Topstitch the white pre-gathered lace around the collar's edge. Stitch or hot glue the pearl trim, then the red braid over the raw edges.

Finishing Touches

1. Cut a neck hole in the collar and sleeve to match the drilled neck hole in the wreath.

2. Insert the doll head neck through the collar and attach the vinyl doll head to the wreath as directed on page 7.

3. Bend a piece of florist wire in half and insert it in the straw wreath behind the collar to help support the collar. Hot glue the wire to the wreath but not to the collar.

4. To make the ribbon ruff, wrap the wired ribbon over and under your fingers until all the ribbon has been pleated. Run a gathering stitch through one end of the ribbon and secure it around the doll's neck. Tie off the thread and shape the ribbon ruff into even loops.

Tray of Tarts

1. These tarts made from Dap-Tex Insulation Foam look good enough to eat… but don't! Follow the instructions on the can and fill 13 (a baker's dozen) cupcake papers. Be sure to end the top in a point like soft-serve ice cream. Sprinkle with white glitter "sugar" while wet. Allow to dry overnight.

2. Once dry, hot glue the various buttons and candies to each cupcake to make them look yummy. The buttons and candies can be slightly sunk into the dry Dap-Tex.

3. Edge the cardboard cake circle with the remaining pre-gathered lace. Secure the lace to the cardboard with hot glue.

4. Position tarts around the perimeter of the circle, allowing the lace to show (put your favorite tarts in front!). Hot glue a spray can lid in the middle of the cardboard toward the back edge and continue piling the tarts into a point by balancing them on the spray can lid and each other. Hot glue them in place.

5. Fill in and adorn the rest of the tray with other candies and glittered hearts in shades of pink and red.

6. Spray the entire tray of tarts with a light coating of clear sealant and add extra glitter.

Wreath Wreminder
The Dap-Tex will "rise" and expand a bit, so don't overfill the cupcake papers. Also, be careful handling these light-as-air "confections," as they will crush easily. If this happens, make more. One can of Dap-Tex will keep you in tarts for the next year!

Wreath Wreminder
Use plenty of hot glue on the cupcake papers, as they have a very thin coat of wax and are sometimes difficult to adhere!

Did You Know?
The Queen of Hearts on a deck of playing cards is the image of England's Queen Elizabeth of York whose son was the infamous Henry VIII! She holds a flowery symbol in her hands representing the War of the Roses.

March
Leapin' Leprechauns

As our flag floats out on the breeze
Memories fly back to me keen
For again I'm a lass, gathering shamrocks
In a frock all made in green.

Appropriately hidden in a wooded glen, these three merry men are busy hiding their crocks o' gold from each other.

For each leprechaun you will need:

- 10" straw wreath
- 3"-4" porcelain Santa/elf mask
- Styrofoam ball to fit inside mask
- pkg. natural curly lamb's wool for hair
- orange acrylic paint
- doll-size top hat
- 14" Santa doll belt
- 1/3 yd. green woven fabric, 60"-wide (wool or houndstooth are best)
- 2 mottled green and brown felt squares
- 2 gold buttons, 1/2"
- 1-1/2" wooden dowel, 5"-long
- drill and 1-1/2" bit
- flocked green shamrock picks (only available near St. Patrick's day)
- assortment of small frogs, birds, nests, and beetles
- assortment of flora and fauna (we used hydrangeas, roses, berries, feathers, and mushrooms in shades of green and brown)

Wreath Wreminder

If you cannot find faces similar to the ones we used, a good alternative is head #ST904 from Designs by Dian (see Wreathsources, page 48). This head comes with its own fake fur beard, which is easily removed if you prefer to use lamb's wool.

Instructions

1. Prepare the wreath as directed on page 5.

2. Prepare the porcelain mask for mounting as directed on page 7.

Hat and Head

1. Cut the Santa belt in half at the back and fit it around the top hat as a hatband. Trim off the excess ends and hot glue the belt in place. Tuck feathers and flowers in the buckled hatband.

2. Pull small wisps and curls from the lamb's wool and glue them around the sides of the head.

3. Hot glue the hat onto the mask face and Styrofoam ball at a rakish angle, covering the ends of the lamb's wool and the rest of the Styrofoam ball. The masks we used came with beards and mustaches and even spectacles! Little eyeglasses are readily available at most craft stores should you need them. We added more lamb's wool curls to the beards and mustaches to fill them out a bit.

4. Slightly dilute orange paint in a bowl and color the tips of the lamb's wool with paint. These guys are old now, but in their youth you just know they had flaming red hair!

5. Set the head aside.

Sleeve, Cuffs, and Shawl

1. Refer to the instructions for making an unlined tube sleeve on page 8 and make a tube sleeve from green woven fabric. Or, use the sweater knit sleeve instructions on page 9.

2. Trace or photocopy the pattern for the Leapin' Leprechauns Cuff on page 39 and cut two from green mottled felt.

3. Fold the cuff on the fold line and topstitch around three edges. Use a decorative stitch if desired.

4. Slip the sleeve on the wreath. Wrap the cuffs around the wreath arms. When positioning the cuffs, leave about 4" between them in the bottom center of the wreath.

5. Re-tape the cut wreath ends together.

6. Stitch a gold button to each cuff.

7. Make the "leather" elbow patches by cutting small ovals from the mottled felt. Use the oval on the Leapin' Leprechauns Cuff pattern (page 39). Hot glue the patches on the elbows of sleeve.

8. Attach the mask head as directed on page 7.

9. For the shawl, cut a 13" square of green woven fabric. Fray the edges 3/8" all around. Fold the square diagonally to form a triangle and wrap it around the shoulders. Secure it in front with a stitch.

Pot of Gold

The kettle holding all these little guys' worldly wealth can be as simple as a small plastic witch's cauldron or you can make one as we did. Go ahead and give it a whirl – they're fun and who needs plastic cauldrons anyway!

> **You will need:**
> - Styrofoam ball, 6" diameter
> - Styrofoam ring, 5-1/2" diameter
> - black spray paint
> - red and black acrylic Polymark fabric paint pens*
> - saw or serrated knife
> - 30 wooden disks, 1-1/2" diameter
> - Sophisticated Finishes Antique Gold paint*
> - 1-1/2 yd. bright green ribbon, 1"-wide
> - small artificial forget-me-nots
> - newspaper, torn into 1" x 5" strips
> - flour
> - water
> *see Wreathsources, page 48

Instructions

1. With a small saw or serrated knife, shave the top quarter off the 6" Styrofoam ball. Shave just a small amount off the bottom so your kettle will sit flat.

2. Hot glue the 5-1/2" Styrofoam ring (rounded side down) to the flattened area. Use the serrated knife to "bevel" the Styrofoam ring in to meet the seam where it joins the ball.

3. Mix equal parts flour and water to make a paste. Dip strips of newspaper into the paste and cover all the exposed Styrofoam. The irregular texture of the paper strips will make the kettle appear to be hammered metal once it's painted.

4. Allow the newspaper to dry completely.

5. Spray paint the kettle black and allow it to dry. Note: Before painting, make sure every bit of Styrofoam is covered with paper or the paint will eat into the exposed areas.

6. Hot glue the kettle in the leprechaun's arms at a slight angle.

7. Hot glue a stack of the flat wooden disks to look as if they are spilling out of the pot. Use the antique gold paint to carefully paint the "coins" gold.

8. Decorate the pot with green ribbon and small artificial forget-me-nots hot glued in place.

Finishing Touches

1. Arrange the embellishments to cover up the area where hands would normally be. We used pots of gold, lots of flowers, and woodland critters in nests, and most importantly, lots of shamrocks. It's always a nice touch to perch a bird or frog on one shoulder. We found a great pocket watch that no longer works and shined it up to pin on one of our little people. He must've pilfered it from some unsuspecting shepherd!

2. The ladybugs on the mushrooms were made with acrylic paint pens in red and black. Squeeze out a small oval of red paint where you wish to have a ladybug crawling (we put 15 on one of our little friends!). On a separate scrap of paper, squeeze out a small blob of the black and use the point of a quilt pin dipped in paint to dot a head at one end and tiny dots on her back. This may take a little practice but once you get the hang of it, you'll be putting ladybugs on everything, trust me!

Did You Know?
Leprechauns are shoemakers by trade. If you hear the tapping sound of a hammer in the forest someday, you might be lucky enough to catch one! But don't take your eyes off of him for even one second or he'll vanish.

April

Bunny Baby

Dressed in her bunting of fluffy lamb's wool fun fur fabric, our bunny baby is ready for the big egg hunt.

You will need:

- 12" straw wreath
- 4-1/2" to 5"vinyl doll head
- 1 yd. off-white "lamb's wool" fun-fur fabric, 45"-wide
- 1 yd. shell pink felt, 36"-wide
- 1 yd. ribbon in blue check or polka dots, 1"-wide
- white straw basket with handle, approx. 10" high x 8" wide
- 1/2 bag green excelsior "grass"
- 12 nosegays of small silk flowers in pink, white, and lavender
- 3 brown hen eggs (blown out)
- 9 plastic blue speckled robin's eggs, 1-1/4"
- 2 yd. pink satin ribbon, 1/8"-wide
- 2 yd. lavender satin ribbon, 1/8"-wide
- artificial bird nest
- 2 vintage Easter postcards (optional)
- bodkin or safety pin

Instructions

1. Prepare the wreath as directed on page 5.

2. Prepare the vinyl head as directed on page 7. Set the head aside. You will attach it to the wreath after the sleeve is on the wreath.

Hood and Ears

1. Trace or photocopy the pattern for the Bunny Baby Hood on page 40 and cut two from fun fur and two from the pink felt lining.

Wreath Wreminder

Start the sewing machine needle up 1" from the end of the stitch line and sew backwards to the end, then stitch forward as usual. This prevents raveling and keeps the fabric from bunching up when starting to sew. Also, at the end of the forward stitching, reverse and sew backwards 1".

2. With right sides together, stitch the back seam of the fun fur hood together. Repeat with the hood lining.

3. With right sides together, stitch the hood and lining together across the face opening. Trim the seam and turn right side out. Press on the felt side with a warm iron.

4. Topstitch around the face opening 3/4" from the edge.

5. Topstitch the bottom closed 1/4" from the edge. Trim the seam and topstitch again 3/4" from the bottom stitch line to form a casing. Clip open the ends and thread the blue ribbon through the casing with a bodkin or safety pin.

6. Trace or photocopy the pattern for the Bunny Baby Ear on page 41 and cut two from fun fur and two from pink felt lining.

7. With right sides facing, stitch one fur ear to one felt ear, leaving the bottom open for turning. Trim the seams, clip the curves, and turn right side out. At the bottom, fold both corners in at the fold line indicated on the pattern and stitch the bottom edge to hold the folds. Repeat with the other ear.

8. Cut slits in the hood through both the fur and the felt lining where marked on the pattern piece. Insert the ears about 1/2".

9. From the inside, whipstitch the ears in place through all the fabric layers. If your stitches miss some of the fur, topstitch from the outside. The fur's nap should keep little stitches from showing. Set the hood aside.

Sleeve and Mittens

1. Make a lined tube sleeve from fun fur and pink felt. Refer to page 8 for instructions.

2. Slide the sleeve onto the straw wreath, making sure the seam is at the back of the wreath. Turn back the pink lining cuffs.

3. Attach the vinyl head to the wreath as directed on page 7.

4. Trace or photocopy the pattern for the Bunny Baby Mitten on page 41 and cut four from fun fur.

5. With right sides together, stitch around the sides and top, leaving the bottom open. Trim the seams, clip the curves, and turn right side out. Stuff only the thumbs with batting. Repeat for the other mitten.

6. Slip the mittens onto the wreath "wrists" up under the pink cuffs, filling the entire mitten with the wreath ends. Secure with hot glue and quilt pins. *Note:* Be sure the quilt pins are well seated in the straw. You will not remove them.

Finishing Touches

1. Place the hood on the doll's head. Pull the ribbon and tie it in a bow under the chin.

2. Whipstitch the hood to the sleeve in back. Use tiny stitches so the nap will cover them.

Basket

1. Position the basket on the wreath as shown in the photo. Hot glue the mittens and thumbs to the basket.

2. Hot glue the basket to the sleeve if needed. Secure with quilt pins through the straw basket and into the wreath as necessary. Don't worry, these will not show when the basket is filled with goodies.

3. Fill the basket with excelsior grass. Add the bird's nest and secure it with hot glue. Position three robin's eggs in the nest and hot glue them in place. Position the remaining robin's eggs and the three brown hen eggs in the basket and hot glue them in place.

4. Disassemble the small flowers and re-wire them in groups of three colors each. Clip their wires short and hot glue the nosegays around the basket edges, up the handle, spilling over the edges, and among the eggs. Don't be stingy, the more the merrier! (We used flower colors that complemented the two vintage postcards we had but any combination of spring/Easter colors will work.)

5. Finally, tuck some leftover flowers under and around the hood. Make a few loops of the 1/8" ribbon and glue it to the basket. Tuck in vintage postcards if desired.

Did You Know?

The Easter bunny was first introduced to America by German settlers (the same guys who gave us the Christmas tree!) in the early 1700s. The first candy Easter eggs hit the market a hundred years later.

Cinco de Mayo

You will need:

- 14" straw wreath
- 1/2 yd. brown rib-knit fabric, 45"-wide
- 1 pkg. Bumples black doll hair*
- large black mustache from costume shop
- 7-1/2" sombrero from A.D. Velasco*
- miniature piñata, approx. 8" long x 6" high, from A.D. Velasco*
- pair small painted gourd maracas from A.D. Velasco*
- 2 serapes, 8" x 32", from A.D. Velasco*
- black & white pinstripe sport coat, child or small adult size
- white dress shirt, child size 4T
- 20 1" and 2" iron-on floral appliqués from Wrights Trim*
- 12 brightly colored paper flowers
- 18" scrap faux leather cording
- 2 beads for bolo tie ends, 1"-long
- silver button, 1-1/2"

*see Wreathsources, page 48

This dashing señor adds a splash of color to the well worn door of the Avila Adobe.

Instructions

1. Prepare the wreath as directed on page 5.

2. Refer to the tube sock head instructions on page 5 and use the brown rib-knit fabric to make a tube sock head.

3. Wrap some doll hair several times around two fingers. Carefully remove the looped hair from your fingers and place the middle under the pressure foot of your sewing machine. Set the machine for zigzag and stitch down the center. Do not remove this from the sewing machine. Without lifting the pressure foot, repeat several times, adding to the original hair until you have a "line" of hair approximately 15" long.

4. Fold the hair in half down the middle on top of itself. Stitch again down the center line to thicken the amount of hair you have.

5. Hot glue the hair from ear to ear to the tube sock head.

6. Hot glue the mustache on the face.

7. Position the sombrero on the head at a rakish angle and hot glue it in place. Kasey "redecorated" our sombrero with several small floral appliqués. Even though they are made to iron-on, hot gluing them in place was much easier.

Sleeve, Cuffs, and Lapels

1. To dress el señor, refer to the Sport Coat Sleeve and Lapels with Dress Shirt Collar and Cuffs instructions on page 9. Iron or glue more floral appliqués on the sport coat sleeves before putting them on the wreath.

2. Tape the wreath ends back together and cover the tape with a small piece of the rib-knit fabric used for the head.

3. Slip a 1" silver bead on each end of the faux leather cord. Wrap the cord around the neck and under the shirt collar. Hot glue the cord ends together under the chin and add the larger silver button on top while the glue is still hot.

Finishing Touches

1. Stitch the two serapes end-to-end. Gather slightly at the stitch line and wrap it over the right shoulder. Tie the ends together on the opposite side and add a couple of hidden stitches to hold it in place.

2. Hot glue the miniature piñata in the center of the wreath on top of the hands.

3. Fill in with the colorful paper flowers, tapering them to a point. Hot glue the two maracas in place.

Wreath Wreminder

Always save some flowers in case you need to go back and hide any bare spots or run-away hot glue that you can't get off!

Did You Know?

In the mid 1800s, France tried to make an Empire of Mexico under Napoleon III. Cinco de Mayo marks the victory of the Mexican army over the French at the Battle of Puebla.

Cinco de Mayo was photographed at the Avila Adobe, the oldest home in Los Angeles.

Mark sets the stage for a Cinco de Mayo celebration at the Avila Adobe

June
Bride and Groom

Our charming Amish couple took their vows at the historic Wadsworth Church built in the mid-1880s. Today, the church stands on the property of the Veteran's Administration on Wilshire Blvd. in Los Angeles.

You will need:

- 2 Styrofoam balls, 4" diameter
- 2 Styrofoam rings, 10" diameter
- 10 small bouquets of tiny white and off-white flowers
- 1/3 yd. off-white rib-knit fabric, 45"-wide
- flat black doll's hat with black satin ribbon
- pkg. black Bumples doll hair*
- skein yellow yarn, any weight
- crocheted lace doily, 10" diameter
- 1-1/2 yd. white eyelet fabric with finished edge, 45"-wide
- 1/3 yd. flat eyelet trim, 1"-wide
- 1/2 yd. black pinstripe wool, 45"-wide
- 1/2 yd. black acetate lining, 45"-wide
- sheet off-white heavy art paper (used for watercolors)
- shiny black paint pen
- 2 1/2" wooden dowels, 4"-long
- 5 yd. blue ribbon, 1/4"-wide
- vintage lace hankie (optional)
- 1 pkg. florist wire stems
- several straight pins

*see Wreathsources, page 48

Instructions

1. Make the two heads by cutting two 12" x 12" squares of rib-knit fabric. Fold each into quarters and cut each into a 12" circle.

2. Double thread a needle and run a gathering stitch around the outside edge of each circle. Place a Styrofoam ball in the center of each circle. Pull the gathering stitches tight and take a few stitches to secure. Knot off. *Note:* If the fabric is too loose, re-stitch it further up the circle edge.

3. Position the gathered portion at the top/back of the heads. Cut a tiny slit in the bottom of the ball where the neck should be and insert a wooden dowel into each. Secure with hot glue.

Groom's Hair and Face

1. Refer to Cinco de Mayo, Steps 3 - 4 on page 19 to make the groom's hair. Because the groom is smaller, wrap the hair more tightly around your fingers for better scale. Make enough hair for a beard, too. The hair and beard are placed in one continuous line around the head.

2. Starting in the center back of the head, hot glue the hair/beard to the head. Bring the hair down the sides of the face around where the ears would be, under the chin, and back around. Clip all hair loops short.

3. Glue the hat to the head by running a hot glue line only around the back of the hat, where the brim forms.

4. Dot on two eyes with the black paint pen. Set the head aside.

Bride's Hair and Face

1. Cut several 5" lengths of yellow yarn and lay them side by side on a piece of scrap paper until it is long enough to reach from ear to ear across the bride's forehead. Stitch along both cut edges of the yarn about 1" in from the edge. After stitching, carefully tear the paper away.

2. Hot glue one stitch line to the bride's hairline (with the hair hanging in front of her face). When the glue is dry, pick up the other stitched edge and loop it up and over, securing it to the back of the head and poofing it out along the front hairline.

3. To make the bride's bun, wrap some yellow yarn around three fingers about 20 times. Carefully remove the wrapped yarn from your fingers, shape it into a ball, and hot glue it to the top center of the head.

4. For the ringlets, completely wrap two floral wire stems with yarn, gluing the yarn at both ends. Coil the wire around a pencil, leaving about 1" of wire at the top. Insert each coil into the Styrofoam head on the left side about where her ear would be. Hot glue to hold.

5. Place the crocheted doily "veil" on the back of the bride's head so a bit of the edging shows above her hair. Pin the doily to the Styrofoam ball and hot glue a few of the tiny flowers to her hair and the doily (see the photo).

6. Dot on two eyes with the black paint pen. Set the head aside.

Arms

1. Saw through both of the Styrofoam rings and link them together with their openings at the bottom where the hands would be. Use a pencil to mark the intersection on both rings where the elbows would be. One ring will be marked on the topside and the other on the underside.

2. Unlink the wreaths.

3. Carefully saw out a shallow notch where the two arms will be linked. Do not cut all the way through.

Groom's Sleeve, Shirt Front, Collar, and Cuffs

1. To make the sleeve, cut a 32" x 9" strip of black pinstripe wool and a 30" x 9" piece of black lining. Follow the instructions for the lined tube sleeve on page 8. Make sure you cut the fabric so the stripes run lengthwise, not around the wreath. Slide the sleeve onto the ring.

2. Trace or photocopy the pattern for the Groom Lapel on page 42 and cut two of black pinstripe wool and two of lining. With right sides of the wool pieces together, stitch the center back seam. Repeat with the lining. Press the seams open. Place the right side of the wool lapel and the lining lapel together and stitch, leaving an opening at the center back for turning. Clip the notches and curves and turn right side out. Press flat and whipstitch closed.

3. Trace or photocopy the patterns for the Groom Shirt Front, Collar, and Cuff on page 42. Cut one shirt front, one collar, and two cuffs from heavy art paper. Set the cuffs aside.

4. Position the paper shirt front so the top goes over the ring and secure it with pins in the back of the ring. Use two black-headed pins (paint them if necessary) to hold the shirt front down.

5. Fold the paper collar ends down to from points as shown on the pattern. Hot glue the center back of the paper collar to the top center of the ring. Bring both collar ends around front and secure them with black-headed pins. Add more hot glue to the inside of the collar to secure it to the paper shirt front.

6. Insert the groom's head into the ring by boring a small hole with closed scissors points through the paper shirt front and fabric sleeve and into the Styrofoam ring. Drop a small bit of hot glue into the hole and insert the wooden dowel "neck." Leave about 1/2" of the dowel showing.

7. Wrap the fabric lapel around the Groom's neck and hot glue it to the paper shirt front edge. Overlap the ends and hot glue them.

(continued on page 22)

Did You Know?

Years ago, dress shirts were made without collars. Gentlemen had linen-covered paper collars to button on instead. They would stay stiff and starched looking while in use, but could only be worn once, maybe twice, if he was lucky. Heavily starched shirt fronts were sometimes made of linen-covered paper as well. They would be buttoned into place and tucked into the trousers to insure that the gentleman stayed pressed and pretty (and probably uncomfortable).

Bride's Sleeve

1. The bride's sleeve has three sections: the cuff, upper sleeve, and neck piece. The neck piece is a 7" x 9" rectangle of white eyelet fabric. Trace or photocopy the patterns for the Bride Upper Sleeve and Cuff on page 43 and cut two of each from the white eyelet fabric. Place the wrist edge of the cuff on the finished edge of the eyelet fabric.

2. Hand gather the bottom of the upper sleeve to fit the top of the cuff and stitch together.

3. Hand gather the top of the upper sleeve to fit the 7" side of the neck piece. Stitch together.

4. Repeat Steps 2 and 3 for the other sleeve.

5. With right sides facing, pin the entire sleeve together at all seam points and stitch along the long edge. Turn right side out and slip the sleeve onto the wreath so the seams are on the inside of the ring.

Wreath Wreminder

If you are worried about the Styrofoam ring showing through the eyelet, make two more identical sleeves from a soft, white material and line the sleeves.

Bride's Shoulder Ruffle

1. Cut a 36" x 4-1/2" piece of border from the eyelet fabric. Hand gather along the raw edge until the side is about 3-1/2" long. Trim the gathered raw edge close to the hand stitching. Place the ruffle around the shoulder area on the Styrofoam ring and pin and hot glue it in place in back.

2. Bore a small hole through the top of the sleeve and into the Styrofoam ring. Add a little hot glue and insert the bride's head, leaving about 1-1/2" of the dowel showing.

3. Hand gather the 1/3 yd. of eyelet trim and hot glue it around the raw edge of the shoulder ruffle with the eyelet edge pointing up. This forms the bride's collar and hides the dowel.

4. Hot glue a few of the tiny flowers to the front of her neck to decoratively hide any raw edges.

Interlock the Rings

1. Slip one Styrofoam ring inside the other, nestling the "arms" together at the cut out notches.

2. Lift the groom's coat sleeve and push two 2-1/2" nails into both Styrofoam rings to firmly secure them together. Pull the coat sleeve back down in place.

3. Hot glue or tape the sawed ends of each ring back together and wrap a small piece of the rib-knit fabric around each seam. Be sure to work the rib-knit fabric up under both the bride's and groom's sleeves. Secure the rib-knit in place with small pins at the back of the rings.

4. Fold the groom's paper cuffs along the fold line. Wrap them around the wrists and hold them in place with quilt pins whose heads have been painted black.

Finishing Touches

1. Separate some flower blossoms and leaves to individual wire stems. Re-wire both white and off-white flowers together to create an artful bouquet. Include loops of light blue ribbon to hang out one side. Bore a hole in the middle of the bride's hands and insert the bouquet. Secure with hot glue. We added a vintage handkerchief to hang from her bouquet.

2. Hot glue a couple of flowers and blue ribbon loops on the sides of the bride's sleeves at the seam line. Save one or two small flowers from her bouquet to create a tiny boutonnière for her groom.

Did You Know?

The old saying, "Something old, something new, something borrowed, something blue," has ancient meaning?
The "old" represents the link with the bride's family and past, the "new" stands for good fortune in her new life, the "borrowed" represents friends and family who will always help out if and when needed, and the "blue" stands for purity of soul.
In Biblical times it was blue, not white, that symbolized purity and the bride and groom would wear a band of blue on their wedding clothes.

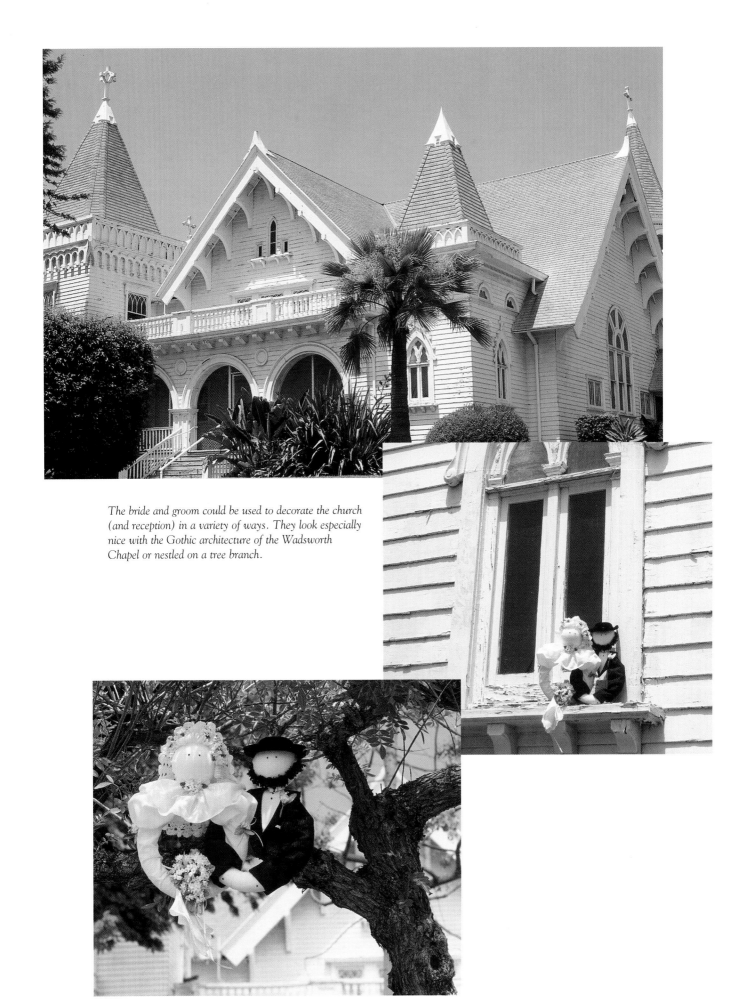

The bride and groom could be used to decorate the church (and reception) in a variety of ways. They look especially nice with the Gothic architecture of the Wadsworth Chapel or nestled on a tree branch.

July
Uncle Sam

You will need:

- 14" straw wreath
- nylon stocking
- fiberfill
- pkg. curly lamb's wool
- pair 9mm blue doll eyes by Bel-Tree*
- old blue sport coat
- old white formal shirt, size small
- 6 gold buttons with anchors or eagles, 5/8"
- 3 sizes iron-on embroidered white stars by Wrights Trim*
- 8" cardboard cake circle
- 6" cardboard cake circle
- sheet poster board
- 1/4 yd. gray felt, 36"-wide
- 1-1/2 yd. red satin ribbon, 1-1/2"-wide
- 1-1/2 yd. red satin ribbon, 1/2"-wide
- 2/3 yd. white satin ribbon, 1/2"-wide
- 3 yd. gray grosgrain ribbon, 3/4"-wide
- 1/2 yd. royal blue satin ribbon, 1-1/2"-wide
- 3 raisin boxes, 1-1/2 oz.
- red wrapping paper
- 5 wooden rocket-shaped bird houses, approx. 2-1/2" with 12" sticks
- 3/8" wooden dowel, 18"-long
- 3 small finishing nails
- 3 each of 4" red, white, and blue paper honeycomb bells
- pkg. silver star confetti by the Beistle Co.*
- bush artificial red geraniums
- red spray paint
- red glitter spray
*see Wreathsources, page 48

Uncle Sam is hanging over the fireplace at the historic Stagecoach Inn in Newbury Park, California. The Stagecoach Inn was first opened on July 4, 1876, our country's centennial.

Instructions

1. Prepare the wreath as directed on page 5.

2. Refer to page 6 to make a nylon stocking head.

3. Hot glue curly lamb's wool in place for the hair, goatee, and eyebrows.

4. Hot glue the eyes in place under the eyebrows.

Sleeves

1. Refer to page 9 to make the Sport Coat Sleeves and Lapels with Dress Shirt Cuffs. (We couldn't find a blue sport coat at the thrift store so we dyed a white one.)

2. Remove the buttons from the sport coat and replace them with gold ones.

3. Iron on the lapel stars, then slip the sleeves, lapels, and cuffs on the wreath as directed on page 9.

Vest and Tie

1. Cut a 24" piece of 1/2"-wide white ribbon and a 24" piece of the 1-1/2"-wide red ribbon. Use white glue or fabric glue to adhere the white ribbon to one edge of the wider red ribbon. When dry, cut this into two 12" lengths.

2. Sew the two 12" lengths together into a point or chevron shape, as shown in the photo.

3. Tuck the ribbon point inside the coat lapels and wrap it around the back of the head/neck. Hot glue the ribbon in place and trim off the excess.

4. Loop the remaining 1-1/2" red ribbon together and hand gather it down the center for the bow tie. Hot glue the tie in place on the shirt under the goatee.

Hat

1. Cut a 5" circle out of the middle of the 8" cardboard cake circle to form a ring. Use this as a pattern to cut out two matching rings from gray felt.

2. Hot glue the felt rings to the top and bottom of the cardboard ring. Whipstitch the outer edges together. This is the hat brim.

3. Cut out a 6" circle from gray felt and hot glue it to the top of the 6" cardboard cake circle. Set aside.

4. Cut a 4-1/2" x 17-1/2" strip of poster board. Make a ring and insert it in the opening in the hat brim. Tape the overlap together, forming the hat crown.

5. Hot glue the 6" felt-covered circle to the top of the poster board strip so it extends evenly around the edges.

6. Cut a 5" x 17" strip of gray felt. Wrap the felt strip around the poster board strip and whipstitch up the back seam. Apply hot glue to the bottom edge.

7. Carefully pull and stretch the top of the felt edge so it flares out to meet the diameter of the 6" circle. Once done, whipstitch the flared edge to the hat top. This will give the hat an old-fashioned top hat look.

8. With your hands, shape the hat brim sides to curve up. Hold them in position until they stay curved.

9. Hot glue evenly spaced stripes of 1/2"-wide red satin ribbon vertically around the hat. Hot glue pieces of gray grosgrain ribbon on top of the red ribbon so just a red edge shows.

10. Carefully hand stitch both sides of the gray ribbon around the top edge of the hat and the edge of the brim to hide the whipstitches and raw stripe ends.

11. Press three large iron-on white stars on the blue satin ribbon and wrap the ribbon around the hat as a hatband. Hot glue the ribbon in back and trim away the excess.

12. Hot glue the hat to the hands and fill in around the hat with the red geraniums hot glued in place.

Firecracker Boxes, Rockets, and Firecracker

1. Wrap the empty raisin boxes with red paper and glue patriotic photocopies to the boxes (see page 44 for art to copy). Hot glue the wrapped boxes to the wreath, two on one side, one on the other.

2. Cut the wooden dowel into three 6" lengths and spray paint the dowel pieces and the wooden birdhouses red. Pound a small finishing nail into the top of each dowel and paint the nail white to look like a wick.

3. Hot glue the three dowels together.

4. Spray all the fireworks with red glitter spray and hot glue them in the arrangement (refer to the photo for placement). When placing the birdhouses, be sure the openings face the back.

Finishing Touches

1. Carefully hot glue the honeycomb bells in place at the bottom of the arrangement and use white glue to sprinkle the silver star confetti all about.

2. We made Uncle Sam's boutonniere from a leftover red silk rose and a bit of white forget-me-not.

Did You Know?

There might really have been an Uncle Sam. Most likely he was named after Samuel Wilson, born September 13, 1766. During the War of 1812, Sam Wilson supplied the army with meat in boxes marked "U.S." Apparently many joked that the meat had come from "Uncle Sam" Wilson.

Here Uncle Sam hangs on the headboard of a bed that once belonged to a son of Abraham Lincoln.

August

Miss Liberty

The Veteran's Memorial Park honors veterans of all wars, as far back as the Civil War.

You will need:

- 14" straw wreath
- hard plastic mask face blank
- Styrofoam ball, 6" diameter
- 3/4" wooden dowel, 7"-long
- white glue
- skein yarn (any weight and color)
- batting
- 6 18" lengths florist wire.
- 2 yd. muslin, 45"-wide
- 8 oz. Aleene's Stiffener and Draping Liquid*
- thin cardboard (such as comes in laundered shirts)
- can green spray paint by Hammerite*
- 8 oz. Modern Options Verdi Gris kit*
- old book, approx. 5" x 7"
- 15 silk roses with leaves (any color)
- plastic flashlight
- 1/2 yd. fancy crocheted lace trim, 1"-wide
- 1 yd. woven gimp trim, 1/2"-wide
- 1/8 yd. clear vinyl sheeting
- 1 sheet yellow tissue paper
- foam paint brush

*see Wreathsources, page 48

Miss Liberty shines in the Veteran's Memorial Park in Los Angeles, reminding us of the true cost of "liberty and justice for all."

Instructions

1. Prepare the wreath as directed on page 5.

2. Prepare the mask head as directed on page 7. Don't attach the head to the wreath yet.

3. Measure up the wreath's right arm about halfway and cut all the way through. Re-tape this wreath section back onto the wreath at a right angle (see photo). Remember, Miss Liberty has to hold that torch up as high as she can!

Liberty's Hair

1. Pinch end of the yarn between your thumb and forefinger and wind 30 loops from your elbow to your hand. Cut the yarn end and lay the looped yarn aside. Repeat.

2. Straighten out both sets of loops, placing the strands side-by-side lengthwise and about 5"-wide. Lay one set of loops on top of the other and machine stitch both layers together at one end. Clip the stitched loops close to the stitch line. The stitch line forms the center part in her hair.

3. Open the yarn out so half is on each side of the center part. Fold the front edge of the part under about 1" and glue it to the center top of the head, being sure it comes down on her forehead and covers the mask edge.

4. Cut all the hanging loops open.

5. Form a small roll of batting and, beginning at the end of one side, carefully roll the hair up and hot glue it to the edge of the mask Gibson Girl style. Repeat with the other side.

6. Hot glue all the loose yarn ends to the back of the head.

7. To make the curls, tightly wrap yarn around the 18" lengths of florist wire, securing both ends with a dab of hot glue.

8. Coil the yarn-covered wire stems around a pencil, leaving a 1" tail. Slide the coil off the pencil. Repeat with each wire stem.

9. Bind three coiled curls together, two in the back and one in front, by wrapping more yarn around the three tails. Pull the two coils down in back, slightly lengthening them so they hang longer than the one in front.

10. Use a pencil point to bore a small hole on each side of Miss Liberty's head where the "Gibson" rolls end. Hot glue a set of curls, short in the front, to each side of the head.

Crown

1. Trace or photocopy the four patterns for the Miss Liberty Crown on pages 45-46 and cut the pieces out of thin cardboard. Cut seven of the Crown Points and one of each of the other pieces.

2. Hot glue the front arch piece to the back arch piece. Hot glue the bottom edging to the front arch. Hot glue the seven crown points evenly across the top, starting in the center and working down each side.

3. Shape the crown by curving it slightly to fit on the head behind the hair rolls. Work quilt pins through the cardboard and embed them in the Styrofoam ball. Secure with hot glue.

4. Carefully bend the crown points down in front so they protrude at an angle from the head. Hold them in place until the cardboard retains the shape. Set the head aside.

Sleeves

1. Use the Bow Tie Sleeve pattern and instructions on page 8 to make an *unlined* muslin sleeve for Miss Liberty. (Because this sleeve will be covered with a paint finish, it does not need to be lined.) The sleeve dimensions start at 12" tapered up to 18" across the entire two yards of muslin. Miss Liberty's sleeve should be twice as long as a regular bow tie sleeve to allow for the draping. Do not put the sleeve on the wreath yet.

2. Cut a piece of muslin from the leftover scraps and tightly wrap the extended torch arm on the wreath, creating as few wrinkles as possible. Use quilt pins to hold.

3. In a large bowl, slightly dilute the fabric stiffener with 1-1/2 oz. water (just under 1/4 of Aleene's 8 oz. bottle). *Note:* It's best to do this outdoors. Things can get a bit messy.

4. Dip the entire sleeve until it has soaked up all of the solution. Gather the sleeve up as you would a ladies stocking and slip it onto the wreath. Continue to gather and drape the fabric from "wrist" to "wrist," allowing the fabric to puddle in the elbow of the torch arm.

5. Cover a porch railing, door, or board leaned against a wall with aluminum foil for protection and hang the wreath on a bent coat hanger to dry overnight.

6. Once dry, remove the wreath (and any stuck foil) from the hanger and insert the head in the wreath. Hot glue it to the wreath and sleeve. It helps to have a couple of 2" nails handy to push into the Styrofoam ball and wreath to hold the head securely in place.

Torch

1. Miss Liberty's torch is a re-dressed flashlight. Put the batteries in and make sure it lights.

2. Trace or photocopy the pattern for the Miss Liberty Torch Base on page 44 and cut two from cardboard.

3. Cut one 1-1/2" x 13" cardboard strip and form it into a circle. Overlap the ends of the strip and hot glue them together. Hot glue the two circles to the top and bottom of the strip to form the torch's platform.

4. In a bowl, slightly dilute the fabric stiffener with water and dip the 1" lace until it's completely submersed. Remove and lay flat to dry. Hot glue the lace to the top edge of the platform so it stands straight up.

5. Cover the lace edge and the bottom edge of the platform by hot gluing the gimp around it.

6. Hot glue the platform to the top of the flashlight.

7. Trace or photocopy the pattern for the Miss Liberty Torch Flame on page 46 and cut two from the clear vinyl sheeting. Hot glue the two flame pieces together, leaving the bottom open. Trim the edges of the flame evenly.

8. Crinkle a small piece of yellow tissue paper into the pocket formed by the two flame pieces and set aside.

9. Using needle nose pliers, pull the straw out of the extended wreath arm about 2" deep. Work the flashlight into the hole. Once you are satisfied with the fit, remove the flashlight and pour in hot glue. Insert the flashlight into the wreath so it points straight up. Hold in place until the glue dries.

10. Hot glue the book to the left side of the wreath, covering the wrist and the fact she has no hands!

11. Pull the rose heads and leaves from their stems. Create a swag by first hot gluing them across the bottom of the book and around the base of the torch. Join these by hot gluing a leftover rose stem from arm to arm. Cover the stem with more roses and fill in around the flowers with as many leaves as necessary.

Finishing Touches

1. To finish, spray the entire wreath with the green spray paint and allow to dry. (The Hammerite paint actually gives a hammered metal look when dry.)

2. Once dry, follow the directions on the Verdi Gris kit and paint Miss Liberty with the copper metallic surfacer followed by the Verdi Gris solution. We used one application instead of the recommended two. Be sure to get the solution into all the rose petals, hair curls, leaves, and crown arches.

Wreath Wreminder

To make applying the Verdi Gris easier, we filled a spray bottle with the solution and sprayed it on rather than painting it. It gets in all the crevices better this way. If you miss a spot (only noticeable once it has dried), go back and repeat the above steps on those spots. It's ok if a little of the light green paint shows through.

Did You Know?

"Liberty Enlightening the World" by Frederic Auguste Bartholdi, is the actual name for the Statue of Liberty. Gustave Eiffel (of Eiffel Tower fame) created the structural framework for this gift from France to honor the first centennial of the United States. She stands 151' 1" tall (not including the pedestal) and her nose is 4' 6" long!

September

School Ma'arm

You will need:

- 14" straw wreath
- nylon stocking
- fiberfill
- skein gray yarn
- pre-made lace Peter Pan collar
- red paint pen for fabric
- spray of small pink roses
- artificial apple
- 3 old books (approx. 4" x 6")
- old belt
- 5" x 7" slate board
- 2 yellow pencils
- 1/3 yd. calico print fabric, 45"-wide
- 1-1/4 yd. flat lace trim, 3"-wide (or 3/4 yd. pre-gathered)
- pair small doll glasses
- 1/2 yd. pink ribbon, 1"-wide

"I wrote on your slate, 'I love you, Joe' when we were a couple of kids!"
Remember that line from the old school song? We sure did. In fact we sang chorus after chorus of it while making this project.

Instructions

1. Prepare the wreath as directed on page 5.

2. Refer to the instructions on page 6 to make the nylon stocking head.

3. Create the mouth with a bright red paint pen. Paint two small "humps" on the top of the lip line and one bigger one on the bottom.

4. We chose not to add eyes to the School Ma'arm because every good teacher occasionally turns a blind eye to the many shenanigans of her students. (Add the glasses and pencil in her hair after the wreath has been assembled.)

Hair

1. Wrap 25 loops of gray yarn around your thumb and elbow (like winding up a big electrical cord). Place the loops flat on the table. This will be about 15" or 16" long. Align the yarns side-by-side lengthwise about 4"-wide. Machine stitch across the middle.

2. Repeat for a second set of loops. Again, lay the yarns out flat but this time stitch across one end. Trim the yarn close to the stitch line at each end. Repeat Step 2 twice for a total of three end-stitched hair loops.

3. Hot glue the hair piece from Step 1 to the head with the center stitch line forming a part in the center of the head. Allow the ends to hang. Hot glue the three end-stitched pieces by their stitch lines to the back bottom of the head, also allowing the hair to hang down (one piece will be centered with another piece on each side). Allow the glue to dry thoroughly.

4. Bring the top center hair down each side and to the back of the head. Hot glue the ends to hold.

5. Bring 10 to 15 strands of the long hair in back up and hot them to the center top of the head . Allow the excess yarn to hang in front of the face.

6. Continue in this manner until all the hair has been secured and hides the back of the head.

7. Wrap the leftover top hair in a bun and secure it with hot glue. Set the head aside.

Sleeve

1. Refer to the unlined tube sleeve instructions on page 8 and make the sleeve from calico fabric.

2. Slide the sleeve on the wreath and re-tape the wreath ends together. Bring the sleeve together in front and stitch it closed.

3. Cut the lace trim into two pieces and hand gather each along the bottom edge. Hot glue one piece with the decorative edge pointing up the arm, about 3" from the center cut. Repeat with the other piece.

Hands

1. Find the School Ma'arm Hand pattern on page 47. Trace or photocopy the pattern twice. Stretch and pin a double thickness of nylon stocking to these patterns. You should be able to see the lines through the hosiery. Be sure to cover all the lines. Machine stitch through the stocking and paper. Trim close to the stitch line and carefully tear away the paper.

2. Turn the hands inside out and stuff with fiberfill. *Note:* The hands should be relatively flat, so don't over stuff. Topstitch the wrists closed. Topstitch straight lines to create fingers as indicated on the pattern.

3. Hot glue the hands to the lace edge of the cuffs. One hand should slightly overlap the other.

4. Cover the raw edges of the hand and lace by tightly wrapping a piece of pink ribbon around them and hot gluing it on the underside. Secure with quilt pins to hold.

5. Cut chevron points in the ends of two 2" pieces of ribbon. Hand gather each of the ribbons tightly together in the center. Hot glue these small decorative "bows" to the ribbon on the wrists.

Finishing Touches

1. Refer to the directions on page 6 to secure the head to the wreath.

2. Place the Peter Pan collar around the neck and hot glue it in place to hide the pins holding her head on. Add another pink ribbon bow to the collar just under the chin.

3. Pull the belt tight around the books and punch a new hole to buckle.

4. Place the belt under her hands and around the wreath. Secure it in back with a 2" nail pushed through the belt and deep into the wreath. Allow the books to dangle 3" or 4" below the hands.

5. Hot glue the roses to the top left corner of the slate. Hot glue the slate to the wreath.

6. Hot glue the apple in place (see photo) and insert the two yellow pencils in her hair.

7. For the final touch, we put a small pair of red-rimmed eyeglasses on our rather squinting School Ma'arm. We also tucked a couple vintage postcards about school teachers and an old 45 record of "School Days" in her hands to show that our School Ma'arm is ready for anything!

Wreath Wreminder

We found that by pinning our school Ma'arm's neck at two places in the front, we created neck wrinkles!

Did You Know?

Philemon Pormort was the first employed schoolmaster in America. He taught at America's very first public school established in Boston in 1635. The Boston Latin School, so named because it taught Greek and Latin, also had some famous students: Benjamin Franklin, Samuel Adams, and John Hancock, just to name a few.

Our School Ma'arm was photographed in the Timber School on the property of the Stagecoach Inn. The school was originally built in 1888. This replica was fashioned in 1995 by the shop class of Newbury Park High School using original photos and floor plans.

You will need:

- 14" straw wreath
- 7-1/2" white mask
- Styrofoam ball, 4" diameter
- 1/2" wooden dowel, 14"-long
- 4 pkgs. cheesecloth (12 yd.)
- bag polyester fiberfill
- 8 oz. bottle Aleene's Fabric Stiffener*
- quilt pins
- Egyptian necklace and earrings (clip, not pierced) set from The Egypt Store*
- large (1-1/4") soapstone scarab from The Egypt Store*
- 3 small (1/2") soapstone scarabs from The Egypt Store*
- balsa wood, 4" x 8"
- 4 yd. royal blue cording, 1/4"-wide
- 4 yd. gold cording, 1/4"-wide
- coat hanger
- wire cutters
- Sophisticated Finishes Cobalt Blue Metallic paint*
- Sophisticated Finishes Antique Gold paint*
- paint brush
- wax paper
- 2 T cinnamon
- 2 T nutmeg
- 2 T allspice
- 2 T ginger
- 2 T cloves
- 1 doz. whole cloves

*see Wreathsources, page 48

Covered in centuries of dirt from the Valley of the Kings, our mummy is also covered in spices. The mummification process included the use of many exotic spices and oils.

Instructions

1. Prepare the wreath as directed on page 5.

2. Refer to page 7 to prepare the mask head. Attach the head to the wreath.

Sleeves

1. Instead of a fabric sleeve, the mummy is wrapped in several layers of cheesecloth. For the hands, fold two "hand-sized lumps" of fiberfill into squares. Center the squares on each side of the wreath at the 4 o'clock and 8 o'clock positions. Secure with quilt pins, making sure all the edges are folded under, tucked, and pinned. These will look like the mummy's hands after you wrap him up.

2. Unfold a package of cheesecloth and wrap it around the wreath, starting at the top near the head. Do not flatten the "hands" too much. Use pins to hold the cheesecloth in place.

3. Cover your work area with wax paper. Pour Fabric Stiffener into a bowl (or use the plastic bag method described on the bottle). This solution may be slightly thinned with water if needed. Unfold two more packages of cheesecloth and cut each into five sections for easy dipping and wrapping. Dip each section in the bowl (or bag) to saturate.

4. Squeeze out the excess solution and open up the cheesecloth. Don't worry if the cheesecloth tears or separates – remember, this guy's been drying out in the desert for two thousand years!

5. Wrap the wet cheesecloth around the head, gently conforming to the facial features on the mask. Continue dipping and wrapping the wreath and head in this manner. Be sure to allow the ragged ends to hang off the wreath.

6. While the mummy is still wet, mix all the ground spices together to make "dirt." Dust the wet wreath with the spice mixture and allow it to dry. We set our mummy outside on a chair in an upright position so the air could circulate around him.

7. Cut the remaining package of cheesecloth into shreds. Soak the pieces in the stiffener and wrap the mummy one last time. Let the shreds hang in all directions. Place small scraps strategically over the face at the chin and forehead.

8. Tuck whole cloves randomly in your mummy.

Wreath Wreminder

The best way to remove excess spice is to wait until your mummy is completely dry, then vacuum lightly with a brush attachment.

Jewelry

1. We started with a necklace, matching earrings, and four scarabs (one large, three small) then "doctored" the necklace by hot gluing the large scarab to the bottom center of the necklace and the two small scarabs on either side. Dangle one of the earrings from the large scarab.

2. For the forehead piece, glue the third small scarab to the remaining earring and clip it onto the mummy's forehead.

Crook and Flail

1. To make the crook, clip the hanger part off the coat hanger with wire cutters. Straighten the bends and curve the top into a shepherd's hook.

2. Hot glue both the gold and blue cording to the bottom and slowly twist the cords simultaneously around the wire, making sure they stay in line. Hot glue the cording to the wire as you go. Set aside to dry.

3. For the flail, trace or photocopy the pattern for the Mum's the Word Flail on page 47 and cut it from balsa wood. Paint the stripes on the front and back as shown in the photo with cobalt blue and antique gold.

4. Hot glue and wrap the 14" piece of wooden dowel with the remainder of the blue and gold cording. Hot glue the flail to the wrapped stick.

5. Use scissor points to poke holes into the mummy's hands and insert both the crook and flail. Secure with hot glue.

Did You Know?

In ancient Egypt, the shepherd's crook symbolized the pharaoh's ability to lead and guide his people and the flail, which is actually used to separate grain from chaff, symbolized his ability to be a disciplinarian.

Inspired by the discovery of King Tut's tomb, this Hollywood movie palace preceded her "sister" theatre (the Chinese) by five years. Built in 1922 by Sid Grauman, the Egyptian Theatre (now owned by the American Cinematheque) was the original site of Hollywood's first ever premiere. In its heyday, movie extras, both male and female, paraded about its parapets in Egyptian garb to announce movie openings and premieres.

November
Indian Maiden

We photographed our Indian maiden in a cornfield near Oxnard, California. It was the closest thing to a 375-year-old New England look as we could get!

You will need:

- 12" straw wreath
- Nakia vinyl doll head by Integrity Toys*
- 18" x 45" leather, suede, or suede cloth
- 2 yd. Indian pattern ribbon, 1-1/2"-wide
- 1/2 yd. Indian pattern ribbon, 1"-wide
- 3 artificial ears of corn
- 3 wooden fish, approx. 6"-long
- Sophisticated Finishes Silver Blue Metallic paint*
- paint brush
- 12 or more feathers
- 12 or more autumn leaves
- 6 sunflower heads
- 6 clusters of small white flowers
- 6 sprays of artificial berries
- 7" artificial pheasant

*see Wreathsources, page 48

Instructions

Note: The beautiful Nakia doll head we used is slightly smaller than other vinyl doll heads so we used a 12" straw wreath instead of a 14" one. The Nakia head comes with hair. If the head you choose doesn't have hair, you'll need to buy the hair separately and glue it on.

1. Evenly divide the hair down the back and braid in two braids. Tie off the braids with small rubber bands and hot glue a couple of small feathers to the rubber bands.

2. Use the 1"-wide ribbon to add a headband. Glue the ribbon together at the back of the head. The addition of the perfect feather finishes this part off. Set the head aside.

Sleeves

1. Cut the leather 12" x 45".

2. Down one long side of the leather, mark 2-3/4" lines every 1/4". Use sharp scissors to carefully cut along these lines to create the fringe.

3. Fold the unfringed long end of the leather over to meet the top of the fringe and topstitch along the fringe line.

4. Hot glue the 1-1/2"-wide ribbon on both sides along the stitch line to hide the stitching and decorate the leather.

Wreath Wreminder

Be very careful when cutting the fringe. It's very easy to start cutting at an angle and leather is expensive!

5. Slip the sleeve onto the wreath with the fringe on the outside (it will lay across her shoulders at the top of the wreath).

6. Add the head according to the instructions on page 7.

Finishing Touches

1. Hot glue the three ears of corn to one side of the wreath with one ear on top of the other two. Fill in around the edges of the corn with the sunflowers, feathers, berries, autumn leaves, and small white flowers. Add a couple loops of ribbon underneath.

2. Paint the three wooden fish with two coats of silver blue metallic. Hot glue them together, then hot glue the group to the bottom of the wreath at the base of the corn.

3. Hot glue the pheasant to her shoulder.

Note: We doubt that Massachusetts Indians wore turquoise jewelry, but it sure looks good on her.

Did You Know?

The Indians first taught the new settlers how to fertilize their corn crops by adding two fish in the hole when planting the kernels. Thanksgiving became a national holiday in America on October 3, 1863, by order of President Abraham Lincoln.

The Indian Maiden wreath is the perfect adornment for a rustic wagon wheel.

December

Santa Claus

You will need:

- 14" straw wreath
- 1/4 yd. off-white muslin
- photo, vintage postcard, or drawing for Santa's face
- 3/4 yd. red silk, 45"-wide
- 1/3 yd. red batiste (lining), 45"-wide
- 1/4 yd. off-white lamb's wool fun fur fabric, 45"-wide
- curly lamb's wool
- fiberfill
- various Christmas greens, berries, and birds
- clear spray sealant
- glitter

What would the holiday season be without a Santa Claus? This one is made with a photo transfer face from a vintage postcard. Your Santa could look like dad, grandpa, or even a favorite teacher.

Instructions

1. Prepare the wreath as directed on page 5.

2. Refer to the instructions for the photo transfer head on page 7. Just about any picture or drawing can be used for the face. Be sure to have the head enlarged to a proper size. You can eliminate any hat that is on the head because you will be making one for him.

3. Hot glue a curly lamb's wool beard and mustache onto the transfer face.

Hat

1. From red silk, cut two triangles 6" x 12" x 12". With right sides together, stitch along both the 12" sides, clip the points, and turn right side out.

2. From the lamb's wool fun fur fabric, cut a 5" circle. Hand stitch and gather around the perimeter. Pull the gathering stitch to form a ball and stuff with fiberfill. Pull the gathering thread tight and use it to stitch the stuffed circle to the point of the hat.

3. Hot glue the hat to the top of the head.

4. Cut a 3" x 13" strip of lamb's wool fun fur fabric. Fold the raw edges under slightly and hot glue the strip around the hat. Add little curls of lamb's wool hair sticking out from under it. Hot glue all in place.

Sleeve

1. Refer to the instructions on page 8 to make a lined tube sleeve. Use the red silk as the outer fabric and the red batiste as the lining.

2. Slide the sleeve onto the wreath.

Finishing Touches

1. Glue the head to the wreath using quilt pins under the beard to hold it in place. Add more curly lamb's wool beard if needed.

2. Retape the wreath ends together.

3. Hot glue the Christmas greens, berries, and birds to the wreath. Santa's arrangement goes 2/3 of the way around the wreath, from his hands all the way up one side. More greens and berries go across the front of his hat brim and a little way down the opposite side. *Note:* One thing about Christmas and Santa…neither one can be too opulent!

4. When the arrangement is hot glued securely in place, spray it lightly with clear sealant and douse with glitter!

Did You Know?

An artist named Haddon Sundblom created our modern version of Santa for the Coca-Cola Co. in 1931. Incidentally, Santa's reindeer didn't have names until Clement C. Moore's famous poem, "A Visit from St. Nicholas," was first published in 1823.

The historic Durfee House, owned by Anne and Edward Dorr, is a bed and breakfast inn in Los Angeles.

Mark and Kasey peek out from behind a column on the pretty porch.

stitch

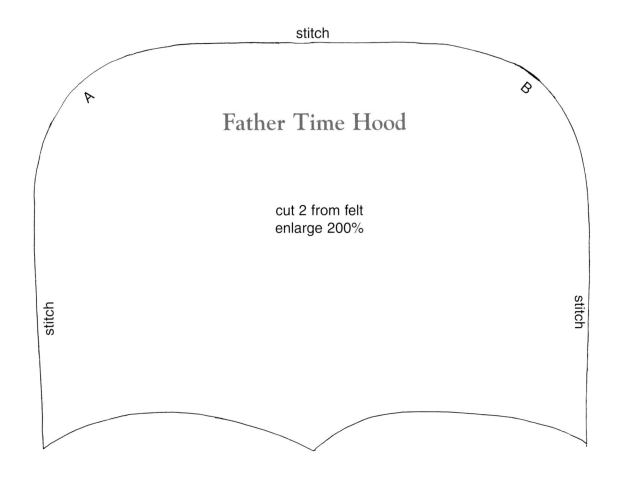

A   B

Father Time Hood

cut 2 from felt
enlarge 200%

stitch   stitch

Father Time
Champagne Label

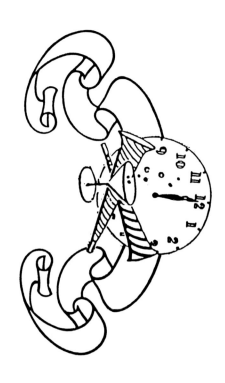

enlarge to fit bottle

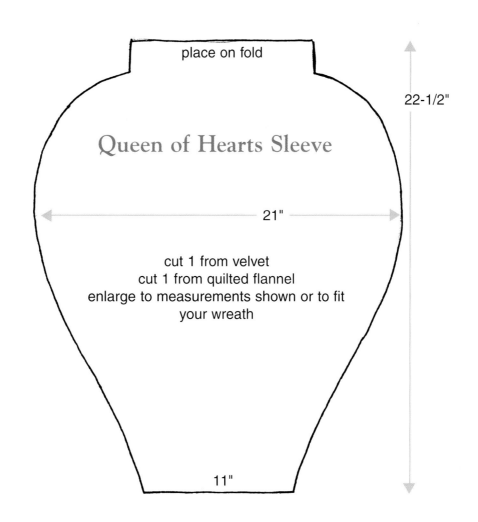

place on fold

22-1/2"

Queen of Hearts Sleeve

21"

cut 1 from velvet
cut 1 from quilted flannel
enlarge to measurements shown or to fit
your wreath

11"

Queen of Hearts Crown

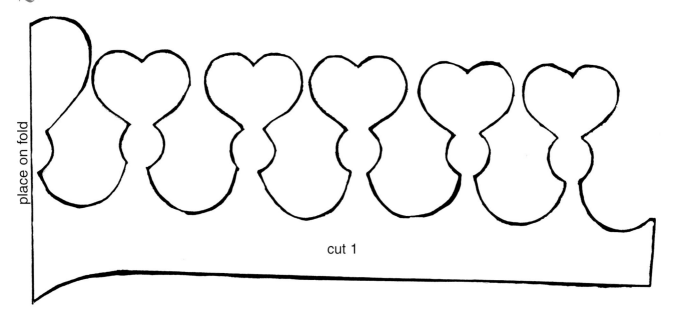

place on fold

cut 1

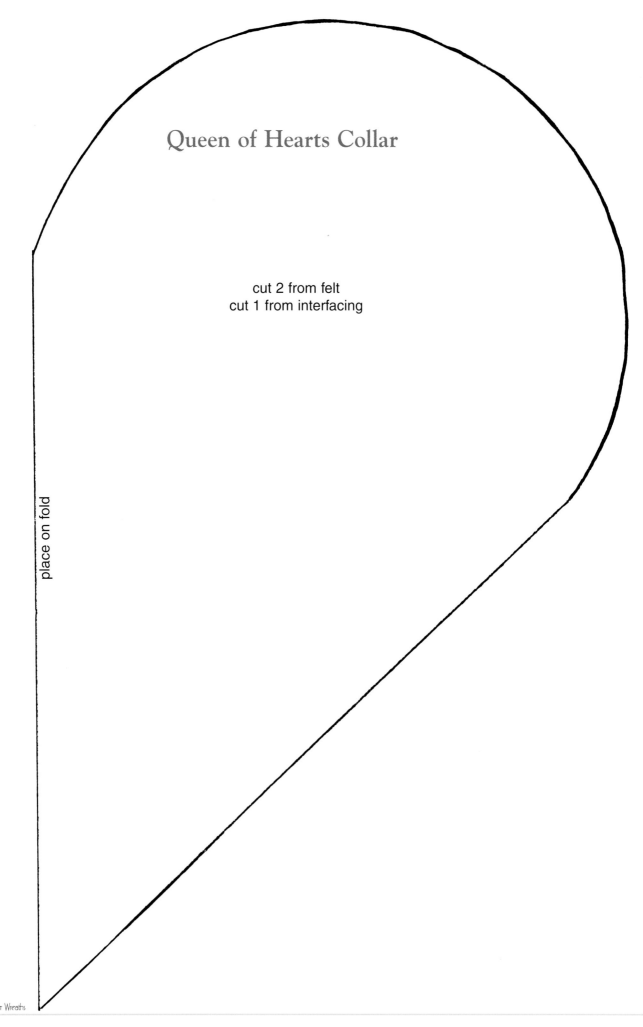

Queen of Hearts Collar

cut 2 from felt
cut 1 from interfacing

place on fold

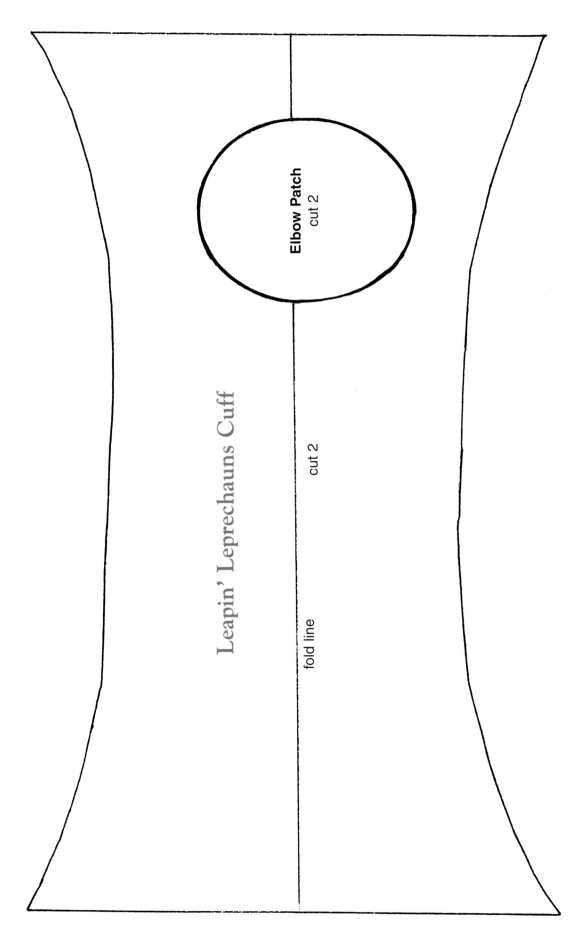

Leapin' Leprechauns Cuff

Elbow Patch
cut 2

cut 2

fold line

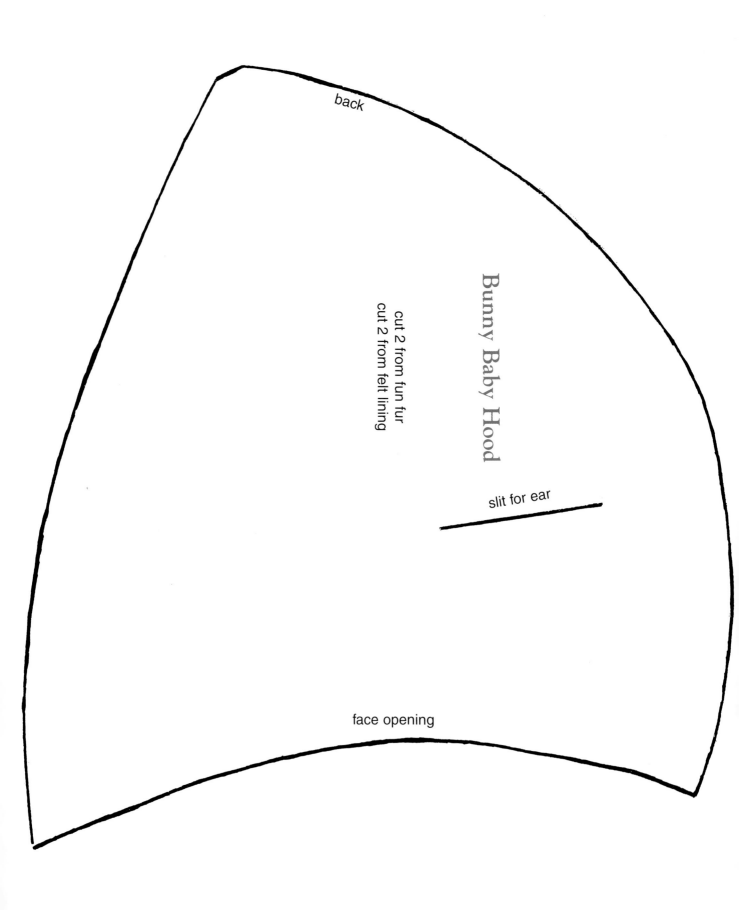

back

Bunny Baby Hood

cut 2 from fun fur
cut 2 from felt lining

slit for ear

face opening

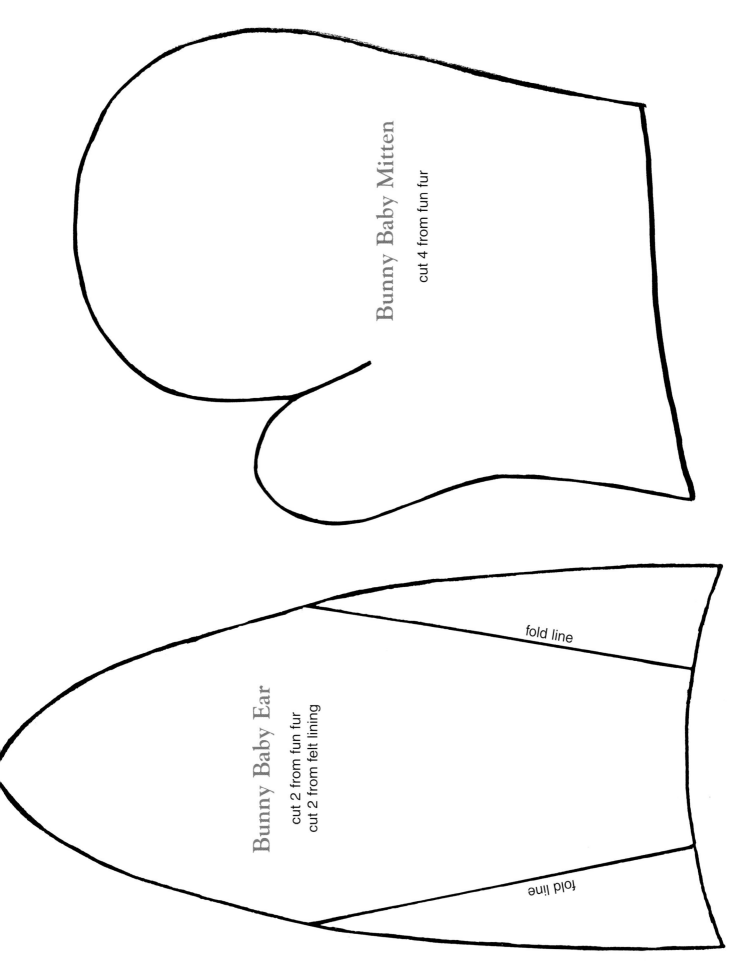

Bunny Baby Mitten

cut 4 from fun fur

Bunny Baby Ear

cut 2 from fun fur
cut 2 from felt lining

fold line

fold line

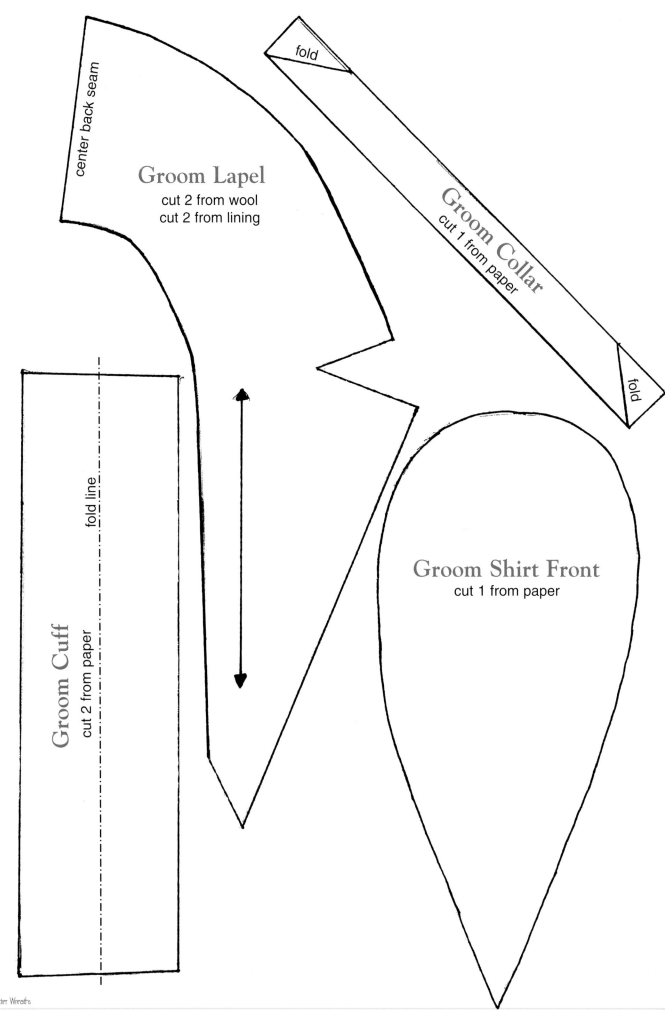

center back seam

Groom Lapel
cut 2 from wool
cut 2 from lining

fold

Groom Collar
cut 1 from paper

fold

fold line

Groom Cuff
cut 2 from paper

Groom Shirt Front
cut 1 from paper

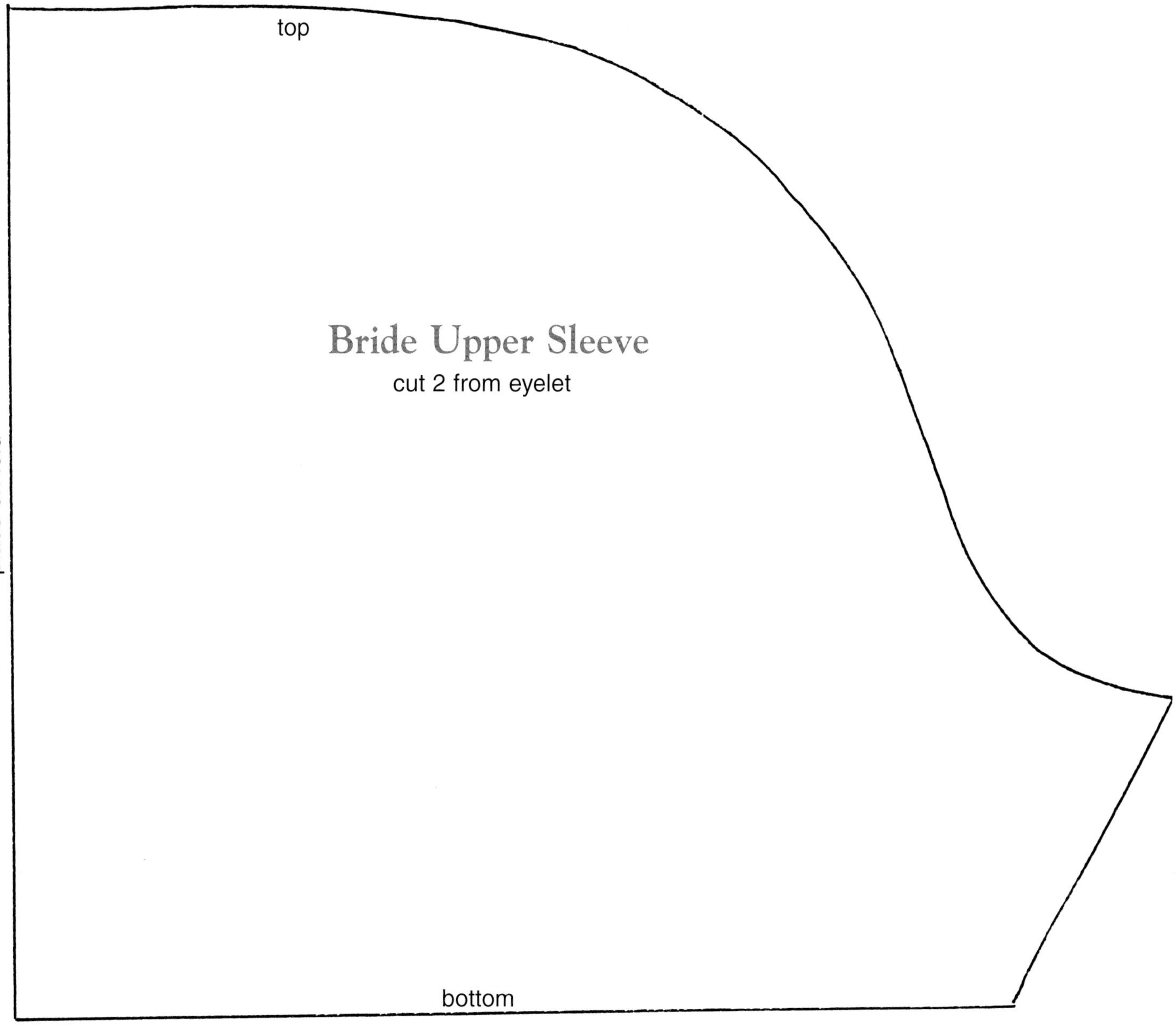

top

Bride Upper Sleeve

cut 2 from eyelet

place on fold

bottom

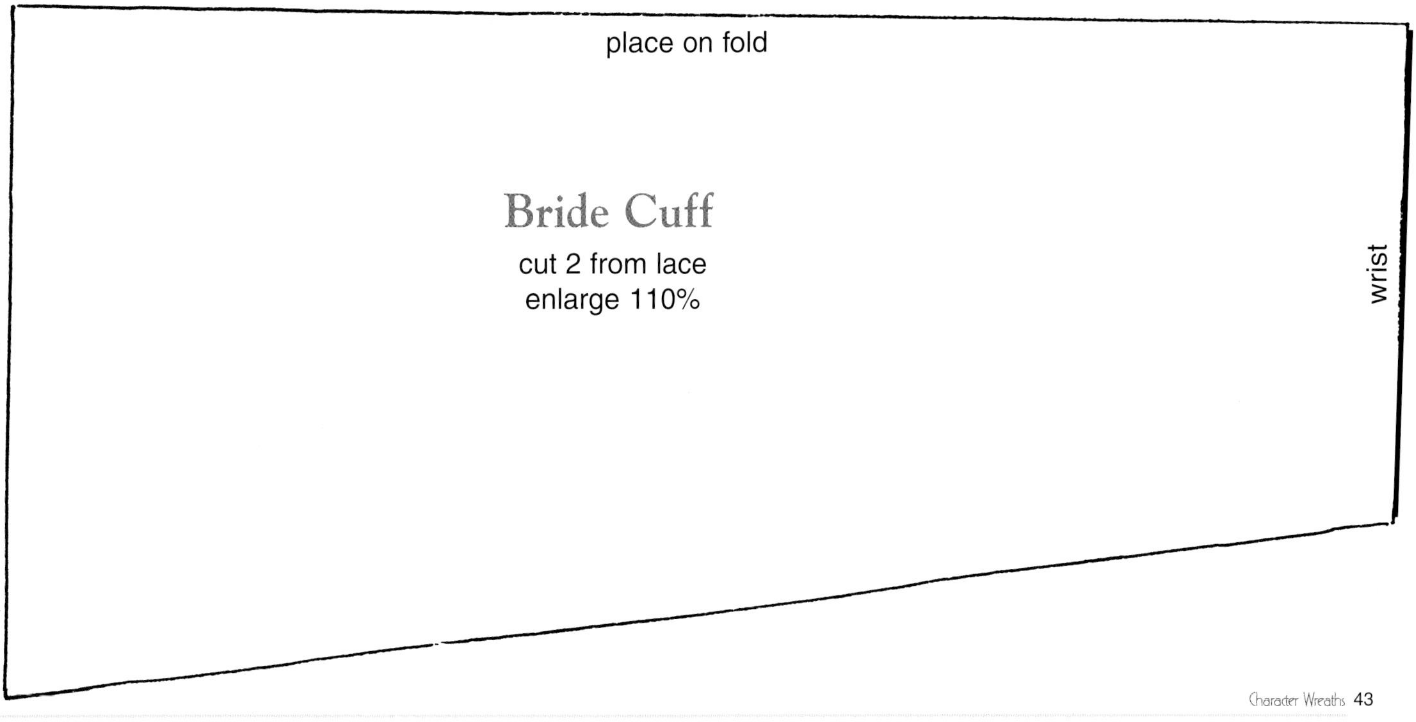

Bride Cuff

cut 2 from lace
enlarge 110%

place on fold

top

wrist

Uncle Sam
Firecracker Box Art

RED ZINGERS

Uncle Sam
Firecracker Box Art

FIRE
TORCHES

Uncle Sam
Firecracker Box Art

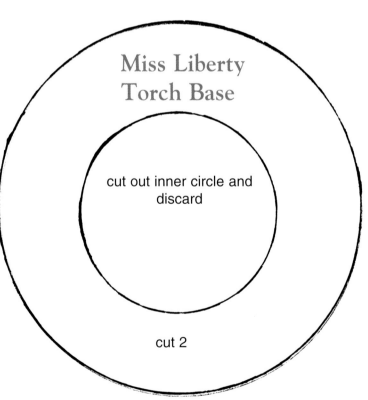

Miss Liberty
Torch Base

cut out inner circle and discard

cut 2

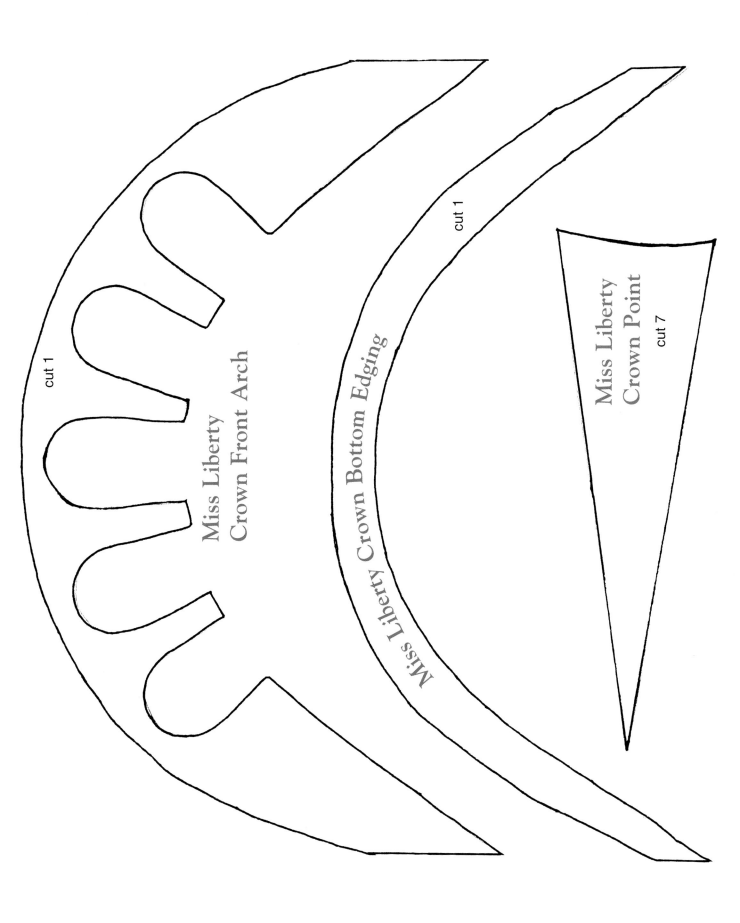

Miss Liberty
Crown Front Arch

cut 1

cut 1

Miss Liberty Crown Bottom Edging

Miss Liberty
Crown Point

cut 7

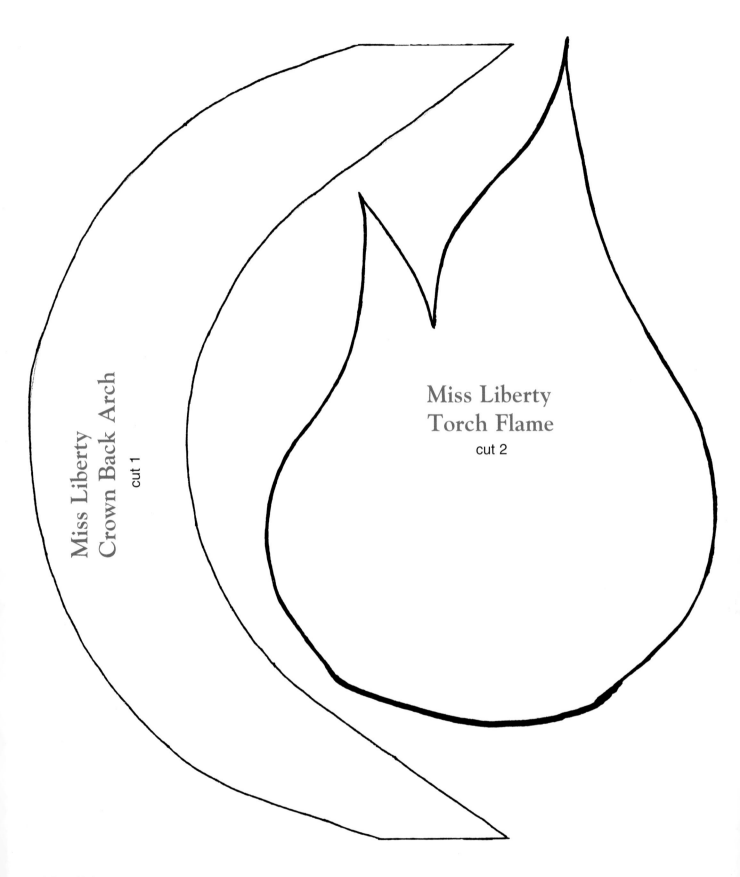

**Miss Liberty
Crown Back Arch**
cut 1

**Miss Liberty
Torch Flame**
cut 2

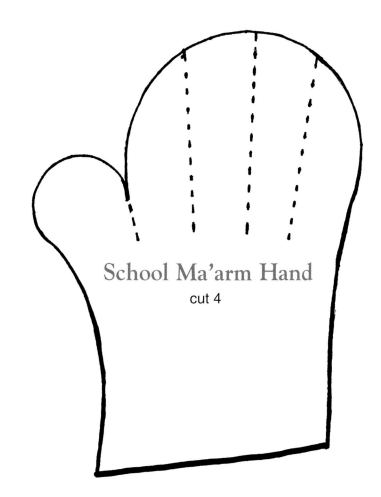

School Ma'arm Hand
cut 4

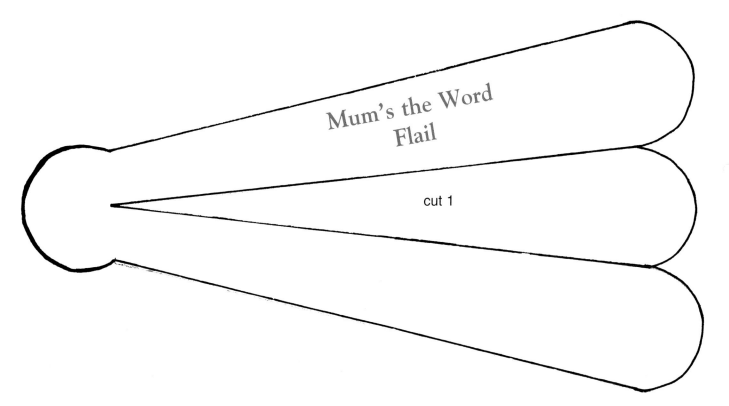

**Mum's the Word
Flail**

cut 1

WreathSources

We found most of the supplies at national chain stores such as Michaels and Jo-Ann Fabrics and Crafts. It takes some hunting and many times in off-season you can find wonderful sales on things! However, just try to find a small black witch's cauldron for a leprechaun's pot o' gold in July! That's why we included instructions for making some things from the ground up!

Many, many thanks go out to all our wonderful suppliers, without whose products this book would have been impossible to create! You guys were incredible.

A D Velasco
14 E. Olvera
Los Angeles, CA 90012
PH: 213-625-7074
Wonderful Mexican trinkets, toys, and gifts.

Aleene's
Duncan Enterprises
5673 Shields Ave.
Fresno, CA 93727
www.duncancrafts.com
Glue, glue guns, stiffeners. Available online and at local craft stores.

The Beistle Co.
P.O. Box 10
Shippensburg, PA 17257
PH: 717-532-2131
e-mail: sales@beistle.com
Paper party supplies available at party stores and online.

Bel Tree Dolly Eyes
Strongsville, OH 44136
PH: 440-238-3870
Doll eyes and "google" eyes. Bel Tree eyes are distributed by Darice at most craft and fabric stores.

Bumples Brand Doll Hair
Available at most craft and fabric stores.

Dap-Tex Insulation Foam Sealant
2400 Boston St., #200
Baltimore, MD 21224
PH: 888-dap-tips
www.dap.com
One of the most versatile products to use in crafting. Available at Home Depot and most hardware stores.

DBD Enterprises (Designs by Dian)
110 W. Hwy. 174
Republic, MO 65738
PH: 417-732-9030
www.diandolls.com
Great Santa masks and porcelain doll heads. Available online. Dian will even paint porcelain heads for you.

Dow Chemical Co.
Styrofoam Brand Foam
Styrofoam products can be found in most craft and fabric stores nationwide.

The Egypt Store
www.theegyptstore.com
Fine reproduction Egyptian jewelry and artifacts.

Goldberger Doll Mfg. Co., Inc.
www.goldbergerdoll.com
Maker of great vinyl dolls. Available at most fine toy stores.

Hammerite Spray Pints
www.hammerite.com
Available at Home Depot and other hardware stores.

Integrity Toys, Inc.
39 Jewett Ave.
Jersey City, NJ 07304
PH: 410-885-5051
www.integritytoys.com
The largest manufacturer of ethnic dolls in the U.S. Available at most fine toy stores.

Kinko's, Inc.
1,100 locations worldwide
PH: 800-2-KINKOS
Photocopies, photo transfers, etc.

Paper Mart
5361 Alexander St.
Los Angeles CA 90040-3062
PH: 800-745-8800
www.papermart.com
The best wreath storage boxes available (24" x 24" x 7").

Polymark Paints
Available at craft and fabric stores nationwide.

Sophisticated Finishes
Modern Options
2831 Merced St.
San Leandro, CA 94577
PH: 800-895-8000
www.modernoptions.com
Available online and at craft stores nationwide.

Wright's Trim
www.wrights.com
Available at craft and fabric stores nationwide.